On
Being
Human

On
Being
Human

by
Ashley Montagu

Hawthorn Books, Inc. / Publishers
New York

To
Warder C. Allee and
Pitirim A. Sorokin
Inspiring Students of Social Life

Library of Congress Catalog Card Number: 66-23178
ISBN: hardbound edition, 0-8015-5508-6
        paperback edition, 0-8015-5514-0

SECOND EDITION

7   8   9   10

ACKNOWLEDGMENTS

Thanks are due to the following publishers for permission to quote from the books published by them:

Appleton-Century Company: R. M. and H. Bakwin, *Psychologic Care During Infancy and Childhood.*

Columbia University Press: Margaret Ribble, *The Rights of Infants.*

Farrar and Rinehart: Erich Fromm, *Escape from Freedom.*

Harcourt, Brace and Company: E. M. Forster, *Abinger Harvest.*

Harcourt, Brace and Company: W. M. Wheeler, *The Social Life of Insects.*

Harper and Brothers: T. H. and J. Huxley, *Touchstone for Ethics.*

The Macmillan Company: John E. Boodin, *The Social Mind.*

The Macmillan Company: Charles Sherrington, *Man and His Nature.*

W. W. Norton: W. C. Allee, *The Social Life of Animals.*

G. P. Putnam's Sons: A. Adler, *Social Interest: A Challenge to Mankind.*

Charles Scribner's Sons: Charles H. Cooley, *The Social Process.*

PREFACE TO THE SECOND EDITION

On Being Human was first published in 1950, and went through several printings. It has for some years been out of print, except in India. In making this new edition available I have sought to bring the work up to date and to strengthen the argument where some of my critics found it weak. I am greatly indebted to the many readers who gave me the benefits of their reflections upon what I had written. I have done my best to make use of them in the present edition.

Princeton, New Jersey   ASHLEY MONTAGU
September 15, 1966

TABLE OF CONTENTS

Part I

What Is the Nature of Life?

INTRODUCTION

To be human is to be in danger. By virtue of his possession of a unique nervous system, a nervous system which is much more plastic and educable than that of any other living animal, man is capable of confusing and endangering himself considerably more frequently. So-called civilized man of the Western world has befuddled and endangered himself to such a degree that he stands today on the very brink of destruction —self-destruction. The atom bomb, the hydrogen bomb, and bacteriological warfare are not the overpessimistic prognostications of dreary Jeremiahs; they are terrible realities. The first has already been used. The other two are ready for use. That anyone should be willing to employ such instruments of destruction at all is commentary enough upon the sorry pass to which man has come.

Such a pass that there are some who say that perhaps it would be just as well if Western man were to exterminate himself; it would certainly be one way in which to end all his problems. But suicide is never a solution to any human problem. It has often been said that the would-be suicide would never commit that final act of despair if he had a sympathetic ear into which to pour his troubles. What must be realized is that every human being is a problem in search of a solution. Some are merely parts of the problem, while others constitute part of the solution. Most of us—all of us—need a sympathetic ear and a solution to the problem which is the meaning of our lives—what our lives are, what they should be.

The problem of modern man is the problem of human relations—of man's relations to his fellow men and to himself. Personal, community, national, and international problems are first, fundamentally, and finally problems in human relations. This fact has been more or less vaguely recognized for a long time, and, indeed, intercourse between persons as between nations has been, to some extent, conducted on the basis of certain theories of human relations—with the results that we all know. For example, the theory that war between nations is natural; that man is full of dangerous instincts that must be controlled; that competition between men is necessary for their fullest development. Organized and secular religions, science, and philosophy have provided a style of life for human beings, but so far none of them have succeeded in solving the problem of how men can live in peace with their fellow men and with themselves. *And yet the knowledge to do just this is today available.*

It is the purpose of this little book to show that science is today in a position to teach man, in the most convincing of all ways, not only that his problems in human relations can be solved, but also the manner in which they may be solved.

During the last fifty years scientists have been conducting investigations on a wide variety of problems touching life and human nature. Many fundamental discoveries have been made, but, largely owing to the fact that we live in an age of overspecialization and compartmentalization of knowledge, no one has endeavored to put all this knowledge together and work out its meaning for the understanding of life and the nature of man.[1] This task is not as herculean as it may at first appear, for when I speak of putting "all this knowledge together," I mean all the relevant and significant knowledge sufficient to give sound answers to the questions asked. This is a task in which I have been interested for many years, and in this little book I have attempted to return answers to some of the questions asked.[2]

In sending this book out into the world, I should like to make it quite clear that, had it not been for the work of numerous other scientists, the present volume could never have been written. What I have done is to integrate some of their more important findings and work out their significance for the understanding of life and the nature of man. There is, perhaps, one original idea developed in this book, and it is fundamental. It constitutes my own small contribution to the solution of an important problem. It will be properly underscored when I come to it.

---

[1] For a recent attempt see B. Berelson and G. Steiner, *Human Behavior: An Inventory of Scientific Findings,* Harcourt, Brace & World, New York, 1964.

[2] For a more detailed study see Ashley Montagu, *The Direction of Human Development,* Harper & Bros., New York, 1955.

The size of the book precludes the possibility of citing more than a minimal fraction of the available facts necessary to prove the points which I attempt to establish in the present volume. I hope, however, that while the work is full of conclusions, it will not be received as one consisting of purely declarative statements.

"THE SURVIVAL OF THE FITTEST"

ALL OF US ARE THE INHERITORS OF A TRADI-
tion of thought, relating to the nature of life, which has
been handed down to us from the nineteenth century.
Life, this view holds, is struggle, competition, the survival of the fittest. In the jungle, a fight with "Nature,
red in tooth and claw"; in society, the claw is perhaps
gloved, and the fight is called a "struggle" in which "the
race is to the swiftest," in which "the strongest survive
and the weakest go to the wall."

It is commonly believed that much of the social
thought of the nineteenth century was determined by
the biological thinkers of the day. This belief is probably
only partially true. It is, however, an open question
whether it was not equally true that the social thought
of the day determined the form of thought on biological
questions.

15

The Industrial Revolution struck England first. Here a hereditary aristocracy moved into business in a big way. Labor was cheap, and employers saw to it that it was kept cheap as long as possible. The justification for employing small children and their parents in more or less continuous labor was that these were *inferior classes* of people who were valuable primarily as labor. There would always be poor people. Starvation was a law of nature.[8]

The prejudices of a class have often been mistaken for the laws of nature, and during this early period of the Industrial Revolution, one great English social thinker, perhaps one of the leading social thinkers of any day, Thomas Robert Malthus (1766–1834), in fact attempted to prove in his *Essay on Population,* published in 1798, that poverty and distress are unavoidable since population increases in geometric ratio while the means of subsistence increases in arithmetic ratio. As checks on population, Malthus at first accepted only war, famine, and disease, but later admitted that moral restraint might also act as a deterrent. This doctrine fitted the philosophy of the burgeoning industrial economy of England like a glove. It is perhaps not to be wondered at that in 1805 Malthus was made a professor at the College of the East India Company!

There can be little doubt that Malthus' basic conclusions were sound, and that we have much to learn from them today. Indeed, unless we do learn the lessons Malthus taught, all our efforts may come to naught.[4]

---

[8] John and Barbara Hammond, *The Bleak Age,* Pelican Books, Baltimore, 1947.

[4] Alfred Sauvy, *Fertility and Survival,* Criterion Books, New York, 1961.

According to Malthus, human life consisted of a constant "struggle for existence" in which the weaker perpetually perished. It was the reading of this *Essay* in 1838 that gave Charles Darwin the clue to the basic principle of his theory expounded in *The Origin of Species by Means of Natural Selection, or the Preservation of Favoured Races in the Struggle for Life,* which was published in November 1859. Throughout the remainder of the nineteenth century, biologists were sedulously engaged in proving the Malthusian-Darwinian conception of the preservation of favored groups in the struggle for life.

What Darwin sought to do in *The Origin of Species* may best be stated in his own words, which are here given from the first edition of his book:

The Struggle for Existence amongst all organic beings throughout the world, which inevitably follows from their high geometrical powers of increase, will be treated of. This is the doctrine of Malthus, applied to the whole animal and vegetable kingdoms. As many more of each species are born than can possibly survive; and as, consequently, there is a frequently recurring struggle for existence, it follows that any being, if it vary however slightly in any manner profitable to itself, under the complex and sometimes varying conditions of life, will have a better chance of surviving, and thus be *naturally selected.* From the strong principle of inheritance, any selected variety will tend to propagate its new and modified form.

Malthus' book had been widely read, but Darwin's swept all before it. Not only did biologists now have a compass to steer by, but social philosophers and, particularly, enterprising industrialists and galloping imperialists could now justify the exploitation of their workers, the maintenance of a permanent pool of unemployed labor, and the expropriation and exploitation of "inferior" or "superannuated" races. Biologists could claim that animals are in a constant state of "warfare"

17

with one another, and that the two cardinal principles of natural selection are "the struggle for existence" and "the survival of the fittest." Even before this, the poet Tennyson had sung of "Nature, red in tooth and claw."

The law of life, according to such thinkers, is the law of conflict. In his "Struggle for Existence" manifesto published in 1888, the distinguished biologist Thomas Henry Huxley wrote that, "from the point of view of the moralist, the animal world is on about the same level as a gladiator's show. The creatures are fairly well treated, and set to fight, whereby the strongest, the swiftest and the cunningest live to fight another day. The spectator has no need to turn his thumb down, as no quarter is given." And again, with reference to primitive man, "the weakest and stupidest went to the wall, while the toughest and shrewdest, those who were best fitted to cope with their circumstances, but not the best in another way, survived. Life was a continuous free fight, and beyond the limited and temporary relations of the family, the Hobbesian war of each against all was the normal state of existence." [5]

To those who wished to have it otherwise, it was of no moment that Huxley, two years before his death, in the memorable Romanes Lecture which he delivered at Oxford in 1893, paused long enough to make his chief point, namely, that

the influence of the cosmic process on the evolution of society is the greater the more rudimentary its civilization. Social checking means a checking of the cosmic process at every step and the substitution for it of another, which may be called the ethical process; the end of which is not the survival of those who may happen to be the fittest, in respect of the whole of the conditions which obtain, but of those who are ethically the best.

---

[5] "The Struggle for Existence: A Programme," *Nineteenth Century,* vol. 23, February 1888, pp. 161–80.

. . . the practice of that which is ethically the best—what we call goodness or virtue—involves a course of conduct which, in all respects, is opposed to that which leads to success in the cosmic struggle for existence. In place of ruthless self-assertion it demands self-restraint; in place of thrusting aside, or treading down, all competitors, it requires that the individual shall not merely respect, but shall help his fellows; its influence is directed, not so much to the survival of the fittest, as to the fitting of as many as possible to survive. It repudiates the gladiatorial theory of existence. . . .

It is from the neglect of these plain considerations that the fanatical individualism of our time attempts to apply the analogy of cosmic nature to society.[6]

But these final conclusions of Huxley came rather late in the day. His "Struggle for Existence" manifesto of five years earlier had summed up the more generally accepted viewpoint of his time.

That viewpoint, especially when taken out of context, gave a biological justification for competition between men of the same community, for competition—and conflict, war, between nations. It justified the exploitation of one's neighbors, one's competitors, and of inferior peoples by superior peoples, for does not nature deliver a biologically just decision?

Herbert Spencer, the English sociologist, was the leader in the application of such biologistic thought to human social behavior. He had early developed such ideas under the stimulus of Malthus and, with the advent of Darwinism, elaborated these ideas into a viewpoint which has come to be known as Social Darwinism. Social Darwinism defines the system of beliefs holding that the same principles apply in the evolution and development of social as of biological life. Hence a na-

---

[6] T. H. Huxley, *Evolution and Ethics*, the Romanes Lecture, Oxford University, 1893. Reprinted and quoted from T. H. Huxley and J. Huxley, *Touchstone for Ethics*, Harper & Bros., New York, 1947, pp. 91–92.

tion's fitness to survive may be measured by war, that supreme agent of the evolutionary process, as General von Bernhardi and many others have more recently held. Hence, too, as the late John D. Rockefeller (who certainly should have known) said, "The growth of a large business is merely a survival of the fittest."

By those who misused it, Darwinism was offered as no mere apology. It was more positive than that; it was a validation, a biological justification for competition. This doctrine has become part of the behavioral equipment, the system of overt beliefs of almost everyone in the Western world today. And so in the Middletowns of today we find it expressed, as it was to Helen and Robert Lynd in the words of a typical businessman, "You can't make the world all planned and soft. The strongest and best survive—that's the law of nature after all—always has been and always will be."[7]

And this is modern man's conception of life: each for himself and, if necessary, against his fellows. In America, indeed, this principle has become enshrined in the idea of "rugged individualism." In other lands of the Western world, it is perhaps not so clearly defined in a phrase, though as a reality it is well enough established. And so, in the Western world, each man has come to stand alone, "an island entire of itself," for if one is not for himself, who will be? Competition is the law of life —have not the scientists demonstrated it? So we compete.

Such is the law of life.

This view of life is dangerously false. Yet it largely motivates the conduct of most persons in the Western

---

[7] For the further discussion of this subject see Ashley Montagu, *Darwin, Competition and Cooperation*, Schuman, New York, 1952.

world. And it has brought man into the sorry state of personal, interpersonal, and international conflict in which he finds himself today.

In earlier times, as a consequence of the Urban Revolution, beginning some ten thousand years ago, there may have been some adaptive value to the social and religious systems in which tribalism, conflict, and marked differences between social classes characterized these societies. But if these ways of life had any adaptive value then, they most assuredly do not now. The persistence of such ideas and practices leading to divisiveness, separation, antagonisms, and aggression have increasingly become as inappropriate and as negatively adaptive as they could possibly be.

The facts of biological evolution, indeed, do provide a basis for human conduct; but those facts, as we know them today, point in a very different direction from that which the so-called Darwinians one-sidedly indicated. Their importance cannot be overemphasized. And it needs to be underscored here that Darwin himself was among the first to recognize their importance and to endeavor to make them known. Whether or not Darwin was outraged by the excesses of thought committed by some of his followers, I do not know. I suspect he was. In any event, as a sort of corrective to the rather one-sided picture of evolution which he had given in *The Origin of Species,* he published, in 1871, *The Descent of Man.* In this work he strongly emphasized the principle of cooperation and stated that "as man advances in civilization and small tribes are united into larger communities, the simplest reason would tell each individual that he ought to extend his social instinct and sympathies to all members of the same nation, though personally unknown to him. This point being once reached, there is only an artificial barrier to prevent his

21

sympathies extending to the men of all nations and races."

In *The Descent of Man* there was much else to the same effect, but Darwin's voice, together with those of many others which had been raised in protest against the crude, muscular Darwinistic point of view, was drowned out in the din raised by the one-sided proponents of natural selection.

The principle of natural selection represents one of the most fruitful generalizations of the scientific mind. It is a principle which at one stroke solved a hitherto bewildering number of problems and provided a unified explanation for the diversity of living and extinct forms. That principle has in every way been fully supported by all the work that has been done since it was first proposed.[8] What was wrong with its misuse was the one-sided overemphasis on competition to the virtual complete neglect of the factor of cooperation. Natural selection, the struggle for existence, and competition are very real processes, but they constitute only part of the story of the evolution of social animals.

Activities which may collectively be called competitive most certainly characterize the behavior of all animals, but such activities are not all that characterizes their behavior. Cooperative behavior is at least as prominent a form of interaction between animals under natural conditions as is conflict or competition. The two forms of behavior, competition and cooperation, complement rather than oppose each other. Indeed, in a very real and significant sense cooperation is a form of competition, and competition, under certain conditions, constitutes a form of cooperation. In what might be

---

[8] Ernst Mayr, *Animal Species and Evolution,* Harvard University Press, Cambridge, Mass., 1963.

called the tough Darwinian period of the last century, the gladiatorial conception of evolution so completely dominated the thought of biologists and Spencerian sociologists—and practically every sociologist was a Spencerian in those days—that the existence of cooperative behavior on a large scale, though known to some biologists, was almost completely neglected in favor of a belligerently misinterpreted principle of natural selection. It was not that the Darwinists denied the existence of cooperation, but that they neglected it in favor of a concept of natural selection which assumed too much, namely, that life was a gladiatorial struggle for existence.

As Waddington has remarked, "The phrase 'struggle for existence' is a catch slogan put over by Darwin, who was a genius at popularisation; but it is not to be taken literally." [9] In the context of life in the nineteenth century it was a simple matter to interpret the phrase as applying to the conditions of life existing between individuals, classes, groups or nations. Darwin, in *The Origin of Species,* frequently spoke of "the warfare of nature." But this is absurd. There is no warfare in nature, for man is the only creature who makes deliberately organized attacks upon other groups of his own kind. Similarly, "struggle" is correctly interpreted not so much as a struggle for existence between animals as the striving of living creatures *with their environment* in order to survive. It is not the struggle against other animals, whether of one's own or of another kind, that is involved, but rather the struggle with the environment. Insofar as other animals do constitute a part of the environment, they are, of course, to some extent

---

[9] C. H. Waddington, *The Scientific Attitude,* 2nd ed., Pelican Books, Baltimore, 1943, p. 159.

involved. The important point to grasp, however, is that the struggle is not between animals, but between animals and the environment, those animals being more likely to perpetuate their kind who are better able to meet the challenges of the *environment* than those who are not able to do so.

In seeking to adapt themselves to their environment animals will come into competition with one another either directly or indirectly, but the competition is not necessarily or usually one of conflict. Nevertheless, it is in this restricted sense that the meaning of competition, which is the synonym for the "Struggle for Existence," has been most frequently understood, even by biologists. This was and continues to be an unfortunate error, for this aspect of "struggle" represented but one form of a much wider sense in which Darwin used the term. In struggling to meet the challenges of the environment living organisms react (*a*) to their environment, animate and inanimate, (*b*) to organisms of their own kind, and (*c*) to organisms of other kinds. In the warlike human climate of the nineteenth century the last two aspects of competition were projected upon the screen of "Nature" and overemphasized to the virtual exclusion of the principle of cooperation.

Darwin's choice of terms to describe the evolutionary process was not the happiest and, indeed, the fact that those terms lent themselves readily to misinterpretation and misapplication has had the most unfortunate consequences. Which once again draws attention to the importance of the "right" word. The extreme viewpoint of the natural selectionists was stated by Huxley in his 1888 article, to which reference has already been made. These views evoked a reply from Prince Petr Kropotkin in the form of eight articles published between 1890 and 1896 in the *Nineteenth Century*. These articles were later published in book form in 1902 as *Mutual Aid a Factor of Evolution,* a work which made a deep impression on all who read it.[10]

In this work, Kropotkin attempted to show that there existed an unconscious force throughout the realm of living nature which is expressed in a mutualism which serves to produce greater survival values for every form of life than would be the case in the absence of such mutualism. The unconscious recognition of this force, Kropotkin endeavored to show, serves to maintain man in the relation of mutual aid. There is an unconscious recognition of the close dependency of everyone's happiness upon the happiness of all, and of the sense of justice or equity "which brings the individual to consider the rights of every other individual as equal to his own." [11]

Kropotkin's book was the first work of the twentieth century to set in motion all those ideas and investigations which by the middle of the twentieth century have taken shape in the principle of cooperation. Kropotkin's work also served the extremely useful purpose of drawing attention to the already considerable literature on the subject of cooperation in the animal world which emphasized an important and much underrated factor in evolution. In spite of some oddities it is still a book very much worth reading.

Lester Ward, the father of American sociology, in his *Dynamic Sociology* (1893), and Giddings, in *The Principles of Sociology* (1896), were among the first sociologists to emphasize the importance of cooperation in

---

[10] For an edition of this work which also contains Huxley's original article, and an introduction by Ashley Montagu, see P. Kropotkin, *Mutual Aid,* Porter Sargent, Boston, 1955.

[11] These views were developed further in Kropotkin's *Ethics,* Dial Press, New York, 1924.

evolution, and, among English publicists, Henry Drummond chose for his Boston Lowell Lectures, published in 1894 as *The Ascent of Man*, the exposition of the thesis that, while in nature there was indeed a struggle for life, there was also such a thing as the struggle for the life of others. In the years since then, much work has been done in this field, so that today the principle of cooperation is in a fair way to becoming established as a most important factor in the survival of animal groups as of individuals.

Some of this evidence it must now be our task to set out and examine.

THE SOCIAL APPETITE

W HILE DEFINITIONS ARE MORE MEANING-ful at the end of an inquiry than at the beginning, it may be of service at this stage to say that by "life" is meant that condition in which a body exhibits the functions of irritability (response to stimuli), motility (movement), and reproductivity (multiplication). An organism is that organization of interactive elements which displays the functions of life in a self-consistent manner. By "social" we mean all those interactions between organisms or groups in which needs are satisfied. By "cultural" is meant the particular way of life that characterizes the social activities of a group.

In the early stages of life upon this earth, it is probable that the only forms of life were represented by single-celled plant and animal forms. In these forms of life the single cell is a complete and self-supporting organism which performs all the necessary vital functions for itself by means of the differentiated parts of its protoplasmic body. The amoeba and the paramecium are familiar examples of such unicellular organisms. These organisms always originate by division or fission of a cell. The parent cell divides to form two smaller daughter cells. It is suggested (with some trepidation, it must be confessed, at the seeming foolhardiness of such a proposal), that in this fact, at this early stage, may be perceived the fundamental bases or origins of social life, the relation of daughter cells to each other and to the parent cell from which they have originated by the process of division or budding off or cleavage. *Omnis cellula e cellula*—every cell from a cell.

In the amoeba, reproduction is effected by simple fission of the parent body into two daughter cells. The plant cell haematococcus (which often occurs in temporary pools of stagnant rainwater or in the resting condition in dried-up mud or dust) multiplies itself by simple fission within the old cell wall, this process almost immediately resulting in the production of four new individuals (the same thing may happen in amoeba). Sometimes, however, another method of multiplication occurs in haematococcus. Instead of dividing into four relatively large zoospores, a restive individual may divide into thirty-two or sixty-four much smaller microzooids.

The microzooids freely swim about by means of their flagella, and sooner or later they come together in pairs, the members of each pair fusing with one another to form a single individual. This is an excellent illustration of sexual reproduction, the essential feature of which is the union or conjunction of two sexual cells, or gametes (in this case, the microzooids), to form a single cell, the zygote, which is the starting point of a fresh series of cell generations.

Whether reproduction and multiplication is secured

by fission or by conjugation of cells gametes, the process is always an interacting one in the origination of the daughter cells or spores from the parent cell. The parent cell supplies the vital materials to the new organism, and in the process of fission there are metabolic and other physiological exchanges before the parent cell multiplies itself into offspring cells, and the latter become organically independent of each other. This type of relationship, in varying degrees, is characteristic of all plant and animal life.

It is here suggested that the fundamentally social nature of all living things has its origin in this physiological relationship between parent and offspring; in the fact that the two are for a time bound together in an interactive association; that the life of either one or the other is at some time dependent upon the potential or actual being of the other. Thus, for example, when the amoeba has reached a certain size, the increase of tension becomes so great that it can only avoid death by dividing, and this it does. The original process of reproduction is a tension-reducing response. The new cells are, at least during the period of division, entirely dependent upon the proper functioning of the parental cell. In this interdependency, brief as it may appear to our eyes, we may perceive the origins of infant interdependency in the higher animals and the very obvious social, and, in man, cultural, consequences of that interdependent relationship.

In short, it is suggested that *the universal fact of reproduction is the foundation of the social relationship which characterizes all living organisms,* indeed, that the primary cooperative act is the reproductive act. Where the offspring are born in a helpless condition and their postnatal care is more or less extended, we have a setting for the development of more complex forms of social life. In the nature of the reproductive process we see, then, the basis for the development of social life, and the suggestion is that social life represents the response to organic drives, the expression of functions which are inextricably a part of the life of the organism.

In other words, the source of the social appetite of all living creatures is traceable to the way in which the living organism originates. All cells originate from other cells; it is impossible for them to originate in any other way. Whether reproduction is achieved by budding off or by cleavage, that is to say, asexually, or whether it is secured sexually, by the conjugation of cells, the process is always one of dependency and interdependency between cells. Dependency and interdependency are the indispensable conditions of life—and these are the conditions which all living organisms strive to maintain. All living organisms strive to be dependent and interdependent, because that is the living state—dependency and interdependency. Because the tissues of every organism "remember" their dependency and interdependency.

Each cell of the organism is dependent for its proper functioning upon the interaction with it of every other cell of the organism. Which is to say that every organism functions as a whole, and not as a mass of discrete, independent cellular elements. The organism is itself a dependent and interdependent whole.

No living organism is biologically solitary [12] in its

---

[12] "The growing weight of evidence indicates that animals are rarely solitary, that they are almost necessarily members of loosely integrated racial and interracial communities, in part woven together by environmental factors, and in part by mutual attraction between the individual members of the different communities, no one of which can be affected without changing all the rest, at least to some extent." W. C. Allee, *Cooperation Among Animals,* Schuman, New York, 1951.

origin and few are solitary in their lives. Most organisms, from the lowest to the highest, normally are to a certain extent engaged in some sort of social life. In this sense there is reason to believe that, with few exceptions, the solitary animal is, in any species, an abnormal creature. Under certain conditions, single animals are often observed, but to assume from such observation that such animals are necessarily "solitary," that is to say, that they spend most of their lives alone, is a very doubtful procedure indeed. The exceptions, such as spiders and certain fishes, are far from numerous. As Wheeler points out, "Most animals and plants live in associations, herds, colonies or societies and even the so-called 'solitary' species are obligatory, more or less co-operative members of groups or associations of individuals of different species." [13]

Examples of what has been called "the social appetite" in the lowest organisms have been known for many years. More than half a century ago, in 1894, the distinguished experimental embryologist, Wilhelm Roux, shook apart the cells of a frog's egg during an early stage of its development, placed the separated cells some distance apart in water, and watched to see what would happen. The separated cells slowly approached each other until they established contact.

As Dobzhansky has said, "A solitary individual wholly independent of others is largely a fiction. In reality, most or even all living beings exist in more or less integrated communities, and the ability to maintain these associations entails some cooperation, or at least 'protocooperation.'" [14] And Simpson adds, "No animal

[13] W. M. Wheeler, *The Social Life of Insects*, Harcourt, Brace & Co., New York, 1922.

[14] Theodosius Dobzhansky, *Genetics and the Origin of Species*, 3rd ed., Columbia University Press, New York, 1951, pp. 78–79.

or plant lives alone or is self-sustaining. All live in communities including other members of their own species and also a number, usually a very large variety, of other sorts of animals and plants. The quest to be alone is indeed a futile one, never successfully followed in the history of life." [15]

When an experimenter removes individual amoebae some distance from a group of their companions, the separated amoebae immediately begin to make their way back to the group.

Deegener, in a series of experiments carried out on the caterpillar *Hyponomeuta*, found that these creatures actively seek out the company of their fellows when separated from them, and that even the isolated larvae tend to seek out their kind. He recognizes a distinct need for association among caterpillars and speaks of a social instinct.[16]

Whether it is justifiable to speak of a social instinct with respect to caterpillars or whether it may not be that a tendency is present which under certain conditions leads to social behavior, the tendency to remain together is a fact.

It is a further fact that, with few exceptions, no animal avoids contact with its fellows, unless such contact under certain conditions happens to threaten it in some way. Under all other conditions, all animals exhibit a high tolerance for the presence of their kind. This does not for a moment imply that a type of social organization is developed by such elementary creatures, but rather that they exhibit potentialities for social life. It should always be remembered that in ascending the

---

[15] George Gaylord Simpson, *Life of the Past,* Yale University Press, New Haven, 1953, p. 56.

[16] P. Deegener, "Soziologische Beobachtungen an Hyponomeuta cognatellus," *Hb. Biol. Centralbl.,* vol. 42, 1922, pp. 241–253.

"scale of life" we are dealing with progressively increasing levels of integration, progressively increasing degrees of complexity, terminating in the most complex of all—in man. Nevertheless, in some very elementary forms of life, such as in certain bacteria, remarkable forms of what can only be regarded as social organization are seen.

As long ago as 1892, Thaxter showed that in myxobacteria a remarkable specialization occurs which exhibits a striking division of labor in the service of the maintenance of the group. Individual bacteria held together in slime join to form a common nonreproductive stalk at the top of which numerous other bacteria join together in cyst-like forms to propagate themselves.

Even earlier than this, in 1880, Van Tieghem found a more advanced type of social organization in the myxamoebae *Dictyostelium*. Here the myxamoebae derived from spores wander about freely and multiply separately. Subsequently all the members of the population come together and form a single aggregate, with the cells still maintaining their individuality. Then some of the cells become immobilized and transformed into stalk cells which are organized into a reproducing mass at the apex. From this position the matured spores become subsequently dispersed.[17]

These are but a few of the innumerable examples which could be cited to demonstrate the existence of a social appetite throughout the kingdom of living forms. Whether we are dealing with fungi, bacteria, or higher plants and animals, the drive to form social aggregates is the same everywhere.

---

[17] For a good account of this see J. T. Bonner, *The Cellular Slime Molds*, Princeton University Press, Princeton, N.J., 1966, 2nd ed. See also the same author's *Cells and Societies*, Princeton University Press, Princeton, N.J., 1955.

Some insects, fish, and at least one mammal, would appear to be exceptions to this rule. Pike and trout among fish, and the hyena among mammals, not only seem to prefer their own company but are frequently antagonistic to members of their own species. I strongly suspect that when the facts come to be thoroughly studied, these seeming exceptions will be found to prove the rule.

If the origin of social life owes its existence to the organic drives arising from the reproductive relationship, it is of more than passing interest to note that, physically, the multicellular organisms probably owe their origin to the same processes; that originally separate cells developed the habit of remaining attached together after division, as the spores in the encysted envelope of the parent amoeba might do to form a multicellular organism. Such an aggregation of cells would provide the means for the development of the multicellular higher animals. Such interactive cells would, by their increasing ability to cooperate, develop specialized functions and increasingly complex relations. The multicellular organism is therefore to be regarded as the expression of increasing intercellular cooperation in which the interdependent cooperating activities of its cellular masses function together so that at all times the organism is able to operate as a unit and as a whole.

With the development of this interpretation of the facts, we reach the view not that society is an organism but that the organism is, in fact, a species of society. The organismal conception of society is today very generally discarded, yet while the notion of society as an organism may be difficult to justify, a strong case can be made out for the organism as a form of society. Every word in Cooley's definition of society, for example, can be applied to the definition of an organism.

Society is a complex of forms or processes each of which is living and growing by interaction with the others, the whole being so unified, that what takes place in one part affects all the rest. It is a vast tissue of reciprocal activity, differentiated into innumerable systems, some of them quite distinct, others not readily traceable, and all interwoven to such a degree that you see different systems according to the point of view you take.[18]

The system which a multicellular organism constitutes can also be so defined. But there is much more to human society than is stated in Cooley's definition, though that definition may serve as a description of society in general. It will not do as a definition of human society in particular because it omits any explicit reference to the fact that human society represents a development of mind, of interactive consciousnesses and the complex of relationships to which these give rise, in a sense quite different from that which might be conceived as possessed by the individual or masses of cells which are the interactive elements constituting the organism. The units constituting human society are comparatively free; those constituting the organism are, for the most part, fixed. The greater part of a society can be destroyed without causing the death of its remaining units, whereas, under similar conditions, death would generally follow in organisms. A person in human society exercises his will in a manner which is slightly, if at all, biologically predetermined, but culturally determined, and his unique being in thought, feeling, and action, again in a manner which is largely culturally influenced. This is not the case with regard to the cells which make up the organism.

All this is not to say that there is no relation between the society of the organism and human society, but sim-

---

[18] Charles H. Cooley, *The Social Process*, Scribner's, New York, 1918.

ply that there is a very real difference between the two forms of society and that one must not be identified or confused with the other. The organismal analogy as applied to human society may be debatable, but the relationship of the behavior of the cells which in interaction constitute the organism and human society is a phylogenetic one, and this is far from being debatable.

Whatever the nature of the factors involved in the cooperation of cells cohering to form functioning manycelled organisms, such cooperation does exhibit the elements of a social act. The suggestion is that such acts originally represent the expression of a drive which has its origin in the nature of the reproductive-dependency relationship; further, that the tendency of living things to form societies is coeval with life itself; and finally, that human society represents the culmination of this tendency, and that in virtue of what seems to be the accident of the development of man's remarkable mental potentialities, his great plasticity and freedom from biologically predetermined forms of behavior, human society has assumed a unique form, it has become culturalized.

The fact that such diverse groups as insects and mammals have developed social life indicates beyond any reasonable doubt the existence in organic life of deep-seated potentialities toward socialization, or what might properly be termed the process of forming society.

Having briefly sketched the case for the existence of a complex of organic drives or basic needs for cooperation in living organisms, we have now to inquire into the manner in which those drives or needs are expressed in some typical organisms, and further, to discover, if possible, what are the biological advantages, if any, of social as compared with solitary life.

AGGREGATION VERSUS ISOLATION

PROFESSOR WARDER C. ALLEE HAS SUMMArized and presented the evidence that among the simpler plants and animals there exists a sort of unconscious cooperation, or automatic mutualism.[19] This cooperative behavior is primarily reflected in their tendency to aggregate, while the biological benefits which follow from their activities are exhibited in the significantly greater survival rate of organisms living in fairly dense populations as compared with those living in sparse populations or in an environment in which they are isolated. Varying with the nature of the environments, the isolated animal will, in general, be retarded in growth or

---

[19] W. C. Allee, *Animal Aggregations*, University of Chicago Press, Chicago, 1931; Allee, *Cooperation Among Animals*, Schuman, New York, 1951; Allee and collaborators, *Principles of Animal Ecology*, Saunders, Philadelphia, 1949.

irremediably damaged or suffer death where the animal living in association with others will increase in size and in the speed of its physiological reactions, tend to recover quickly from wounds, and survive more often.

Thus planarian worms which had been exposed to ultraviolet radiation disintegrated more rapidly when isolated than when they were associated together. They survived exposure to ultraviolet radiation better when crowded while being radiated, and there was a much higher death rate among those which were isolated a few minutes after irradiation than among those which were left together. Goldfish placed together in groups of ten in a suspension of colloidal silver survived much longer than those which were placed in similar suspensions alone.

Allee writes:

When exposed to the toxic colloidal silver, the grouped fish shared between them a dose easily fatal for any one of them; the slime they secreted changed much of the silver into a less toxic form. In the experiment as set up, the suspension was somewhat too strong for any to survive; with a weaker suspension some or all of the grouped animals would have lived; as it was, the group gained for its members a longer life. In nature they could have had many more minutes for rain to have diluted the water or some other disturbance to have cleared up the poison and given the fish a chance for complete recovery.

This latter experiment illustrates in the case of goldfish—and presumably holds true for all other aquatic organisms—the physicochemical basis of the advantage which lies in numbers. Allee's studies on the rate of cleavage of the fertilized egg of the common sea urchin, arbacia, show that, with few exceptions, the rate is more rapid in the denser clusters of eggs than in unclustered or isolated fellow eggs. Protozoans, it has been experimentally shown, grow more rapidly when they are introduced in large numbers into a sterile medium

38

of relatively simple salts than if the cultures are started with only a few organisms. The biological advantages are all in the crowding—not overcrowding—while separation or isolation would appear to be so fatal to the organism that we can be fairly certain that as a way of life it rarely, if ever, occurs in nature.

What is an optimal population size for different groups in nature will depend upon the group and its environment, but thus far the evidence strongly indicates that optimal numbers present in a given situation have certain positive survival values and definitely exert stimulating effects on the growth of individuals and the increase of populations.[20] Thus, for example, Darling has found that among herring gulls the members of larger colonies stimulate each other to commence sexual activities earlier than when the colonies are smaller, and furthermore, there tends to be a speeding up of egg-laying, so that breeding activities are more intense while they last. The value of the short spread of time between laying and hatching lies in the fact that a greater number of young gulls survive under such conditions than is the case where the colony is small and the spread of hatching time therefore longer.[21]

The unconscious kind of mutualism or cooperation which generally exists among lower animals, not commonly regarded as social or viewed only as partially social, undoubtedly represents an earlier stage in the development of social life among the higher animals. It is important to understand in its full implications the fact that this principle of cooperation is the fundamental

---

[20] W. C. Allee, *Cooperation Among Animals;* V. C. Wynne-Edwards, *Animal Dispersion in Relation to Social Behaviour,* Hafner Publishing Co., New York, 1962.
[21] Fraser Darling, *Bird Flocks and the Breeding Cycle,* Cambridge University Press, New York, 1938.

principle which appears to have governed the relations of organisms from the very first, and we have attempted to show that the organic basis for this is to be found in the nature of the reproductive relationship, with the accompanying mutual interrelations which are for a time maintained between parent and developing organism.

At the present time the principle of cooperation is in a fair way to becoming recognized as the most important factor in the survival of animal groups. Summing up the modern point of view, Allee says:

After much consideration, it is my mature conclusion, contrary to Herbert Spencer, that the co-operative forces are biologically the more important and vital. The balance between the co-operative and altruistic tendencies and those which are disoperative and egoistic is relatively close. Under many conditions the co-operative forces lose. In the long run, however, the group centered, more altruistic drives are slightly stronger. If co-operation had not been the stronger force, the more complicated animals, whether arthropods or vertebrates, could not have evolved from simpler ones, and there would have been no men to worry each other with their distressing and biologically foolish wars. While I know of no laboratory experiments that make a direct test of this problem, I have come to this conclusion by studying the implications of many experiments which bear on both sides of the problem and from considering the trends of organic evolution in nature. Despite many known appearances to the contrary, human altruistic drives are as firmly based on an animal ancestry as is man himself. Our tendencies towards goodness, such as they are, are as innate as our tendencies toward intelligence; we could do well with more of both.[22]

The tendentious habit of thinking of evolution in terms of the struggle for existence, by means of which, it is believed, the "fittest" are alone selected for survival while the weakest are ruthlessly condemned to extinction, is not only an incorrect view of the facts but is a

---

[22] W. C. Allee, "Where Angels Fear to Tread: A Contribution from General Sociology to Human Ethics," *Science*, vol. 97, 1943, pp. 518–25.

habit of thought which has done a considerable amount of harm. Only by omitting any reference to such an important evolutionary force as the principle of cooperation, and by viewing evolution as a process of continuous conflict between all living things, can men be led to conclude that survival or development depends on successful aggression. Omitting important facts and basing their arguments on false premises, the tough Darwinians could only arrive at false conclusions. As Allee says, "Today, as in Darwin's time, the average biologist apparently still thinks of a natural selection which acts primarily on egoistic principles, and intelligent fellow thinkers in other disciplines, together with the much-cited man-in-the-street, cannot be blamed for taking the same point of view." [23]

Certainly, aggressiveness [24] exists in nature, but there is also a healthy nonruthless competition, and there exist very strong drives toward social and cooperative behavior. These forces do not operate independently but together, as a whole, and the evidence strongly indicates that, in the social and biological development of all living creatures, of all these drives, the drive to co-

---

[23] *Ibid.*
[24] The terms "aggressiveness," "conflict" and "combativeness" should be distinguished. All drives may be said to be aggressive. Aggressiveness should not be equated with hostility. It is possible to be aggressive without being either hostile, combative, competitive, or conflict-producing. Aggression may be cooperative. It may be defined as the outward direction of energy. See I. Hendricks, "Instincts and the Ego During Infancy," *Psychoanalytic Quarterly*, vol. 11, 1942, pp. 35–39; and L. Bender, "Genesis of Hostility in Children," *American Journal of Psychiatry*, vol. 105, 1948, pp. 241–245; N. Tinbergen, *Social Behaviour in Animals*, Wiley, New York, 1953; J. P. Scott, *Aggression*, Chicago, University of Chicago Press, 1958; A. Portmann, *Animals as Social Beings*, Viking Press, New York, 1961; J. D. Carthy and F. J. Ebling (editors), *The Natural History of Aggression*, Academic Press, New York, 1964; K. Lorenz, *On Aggression*, Harcourt, Brace & World, New York, 1966.

operation is the most dominant, and biologically the most important. The coexistence of so many different species of animals throughout the world is a sufficient testimony to the importance of that drive. It is probable that man owes more to the operation of this principle than to any other in his own biological and social evolution. Indeed, without this principle of cooperation, of sociability and mutual aid, the progress of organic life, the improvement of the organism, and the strengthening of the species become utterly incomprehensible.

We may, by induction from the facts, arrive at a generalization to the effect that the greater the cooperative behavior exhibited by the members of any group, the more harmoniously socially organized is that group likely to be. Interesting examples of this are the social ants, in which the principle of cooperation has been developed to the limit of fixity. Yet, as Schneirla has suggested, it would perhaps be more accurate to speak of *biosocial facilitation* rather than of cooperation here because of the psychological limitations of social ants.[25]

The distinction is, however, simply one of organization at qualitatively different levels. The principle of cooperation has been resumed by a group of distinguished biologists in the statement that the probability of survival of individual or living things increases with the degree in which they harmoniously adjust themselves to each other and to their environment.[26]

---

[25] T. C. Schneirla, "Problems in the Biopsychology of Social Organization," *Journal of Abnormal and Social Psychology*, vol. 41, 1946, pp. 385–402.

[26] C. Leake, "Ethicogenesis," *Proceedings of the Philosophical Society of Texas*, vol. 10, 1944, pp. 7–34. See also a revision of this article in *Studies and Essays in the History of Science and Learning* (ed. by Ashley Montagu), Schuman, New York, 1946, pp. 261–275; P. Romanell and C. D. Leake, *Can We Agree? A Scientist and Philosopher Argue About Ethics*, University of Texas Press, Austin, 1950.

Today, contrary to the "Nature, red in tooth and claw" school of natural selectionists, the evidence increasingly indicates that natural selection does not act simply to favor variations which better adapt the organism to its environment. Such adaptation is, of course, necessary, but the important point is that, on the whole, natural selection favors the cooperative, as opposed to the disoperative, struggling for survival. As Burkholder has stated, "The most important basis for selection is the ability of associated components to work together harmoniously in the organism and among organisms. All new genetic factors, whether they arise from within by mutation or are incorporated from without by various means, are accepted or rejected according to their cooperation with associated components in the whole aggregation." [27]

We begin to understand, then, that from the social standpoint evolution itself is a process which favors cooperating rather than disoperating groups, and "fitness" is a function of the group as a whole rather than of separate individuals. The fitness of the individual is largely derived from his membership in a group. The more cooperative the group, the greater is the fitness for survival which extends to all its members. As A. E. Emerson has concluded, the dominant directional trend in evolution is toward a controlled balance of the important factors within the system. "Human society cooperatively brings the social environment under control for the better survival of the species." [28]

If we would seek for one word which describes society better than any other, that word is cooperation.

---

[27] P. R. Burkholder, "Cooperation and Conflict Among Primitive Organisms," *American Scientist*, vol. 40, 1952, p. 603.

[28] A. E. Emerson, "The Biological Basis of Social Cooperation," *Illinois Academy of Science Transactions*, vol. 39, 1946, pp. 9–18.

The important point to grasp is that, contrary to the beliefs of the "survival of the fittest" school of thought, man does not have to create a cooperative mood for himself to erect over the tufa of his "savage" strivings to be otherwise. Not at all. The impulses toward cooperative behavior are already present in him at birth, and all they require is cultivation. There is not a shred of evidence that man is born with "hostile" or "evil" impulses which must be watched and disciplined.

It is absurd to argue, as Mr. Robert Ardrey has done in his book *African Genesis*,[29] that since man's earliest representatives hunted animals for food, therefore man is a natural killer! I suppose every time I fall upon a steak or a chicken at table this simply exhibits my vicarious desire to kill! Mr. Ardrey's book enjoys great popularity because it "explains" for many of its readers what the root-cause really is for aggression, murder, and war, not to mention juvenile delinquency.

Discipline of basic impulses is, indeed, necessary, but it is the discipline of love, *not* of frustration or policing, which they require. Furthermore, it is not the "survival of the fittest" that is at all likely, but *the survival of the fit*. The "fittest" would stand very little chance under conditions of change to which the *fit*, because of their greater adaptability, would be in a much better position to make the appropriate adjustments.

Insofar as any of its strivings are concerned, the infant of most birds and mammals is equipped with the ability to compete with the universe for attention, and it generally succeeds in eliciting cooperative behavior, usually from one or both parents.

In the process of socialization the energies of aggres-

[29] Robert Ardrey, *African Genesis*, Atheneum, New York, 1961.

siveness tend to be transformed into cooperative processes. The reproductive process is a cooperative one, and, in addition, development as one of a litter or group of siblings represents another early experience in the development of cooperation; development within a family represents a further experience in the learning and practice of cooperation.

Thus far we have been endeavoring to establish the fact that some degree of social life is present in even the lowest organisms, and that such a thing as a completely asocial variety of animal probably does not exist. This would seem to be the first point to grasp in arriving at any understanding of the nature of what is social. The second point is that social life confers distinct biological advantages upon the animals participating in it. Allee and Emerson, indeed, regard as at least partially social any group in which the animals confer distinct survival values upon each other. Thirdly, the dominant principle of social life is not the struggle for existence, but cooperation. Fourthly, the evidence indicates that some form of social life is probably coeval with life itself, else it could not have become established. And finally, the organic basis of social behavior is to be found in the nature of the reproductive relationship between maternal genitor and offspring. It is of great significance that the reproductive process which is concerned with the creation of life itself should constitute the fundamental social relationship and that in the evolution of living organisms, from the simple to the complex, mutually beneficial mass physiological interactions continue to form the organic basis of social life. Man is no exception to this rule, but he is the one animal most capable of modifying it by means of his culturally inherited devices and own social inventions.

The answer to our first question, "What is the nature

of life?" can be expressed in one word, cooperation—the interaction between objects for mutual support in such a way as to confer survival benefits upon each other. Another word for the same thing at a higher level of integration, as we shall see in the pages which follow, is love. Without cooperation, without love, it is not possible to live—at best, it is possible only to exist.

Part II

What Is the Nature of Human Nature?

THE BASIC NEEDS OF MAN

M AN AS AN ANIMAL MUST BREATHE, EAT, drink, excrete, sleep, maintain adequate health, and avoid pain and danger. These basic physiological needs constitute the minimum biological conditions which must be met by the members of every human group if those members are to survive. These basic needs and their functioning interrelations constitute the innate nature of man. Second nature is that organization of cultural conditionings which is imposed upon, and more or less integrated with, the primary innate basic needs of man.

A basic need may be defined as any urge or drive of the organism which must be satisfied if the organism or the group is to survive.

The table below lists the basic vital needs* and may be read as follows: The physiological tension of oxygen

THE BASIC NEEDS AND THEIR VITAL SEQUENCES

			S A T I S F A C T I O N	
Physiological Tension	=	*Urge or Need to* →	*Which Leads to the Act of*	→ *Homeostasis*
Oxygen hunger	=	intake air	→ breathing	→ oxygenation of tissues
Hunger	=	ingest food	→ ingesting food	→ satiation
Thirst	=	intake liquid	→ intaking liquid	→ quenching
Fatigue	=	rest	→ resting	→ restoration of muscular and nervous organization
Restlessness	=	be active	→ activity	→ reduction of energy to equilibrium
Somnolence	=	sleep	→ sleeping	→ awakening with restored energy
Bladder pressure	=	micturate	→ micturating	→ removal tension
Colon pressure	=	defecate	→ defecation	→ removal tension
Fright	=	escape	→ escaping from danger	→ relaxation
Pain	=	avoid	→ avoidance	→ return to normal state
Internal Excitation	=	Craving	→ Neuromuscular Act	Equilibrium

---

* Sex or conjugation is not a vital basic need, since the individual can survive in perfect health without its satisfaction. Clearly, however, it is a need which must be satisfied by some individuals if the group is to survive.

50

hunger represents the urge or need to intake air. It is an imperative need, one which must be satisfied if the organism is to survive. This need usually leads to the act of breathing, a satisfying act in itself, and this normally results in oxygenation of the tissues of the body, a replenishment of energy, and a restoration to equilibrium, homeostasis. It is to be noted that the act of breathing is part of the process of satisfaction and that the replenishment of the tissues with the necessary energy for their proper functioning is the end effect. And so on for the rest of the basic vital sequences.

In addition to the vital basic needs, the satisfaction of which is necessary if the individual and the group are to survive, there are several nonvital basic needs which must be satisfied if the organism is to develop and maintain adequate mental health. These nonvital basic needs have their origin in the same kinds of physiological states as do the vital basic needs. Two of these nonvital basic needs may be schematized as follows:

		SATISFACTION	
Physiological Tension	*Urge or* = *Need to →*	*Which Leads to the Act of*	→ *Homeostasis*
Feeling of non-dependency or aloneness	be with = others →	physical contact or association	→ feeling of security or interdependency
General need or tension	expres- = sion →	communica- tion	→ social recognition

The tension of nondependency is doubtless connected in the continuum of life (phylogenetically) with the parent-offspring relationship which is characteristic of all living things, and in the individual history of the person (ontogenetically) is associated with his prolonged sojourn within the womb. During these phases of its

51

existence, within the womb and during infancy, that is, the organism is *dependent* upon the maternal organism for the satisfaction of its needs.

Dependency is the state of reliance of the organism upon objects outside itself for the satisfaction of its needs. In brief, dependency is the state of striving to obtain support from sources external to the organism. The directiveness of drives is, therefore, outward in order to obtain gratification of needs from objects stimulated by the appropriate acts.

All needs are dependent. They must therefore be satisfied by some object or objects. An attempt will be made here to show that those needs must always be satisfied in the manner in which they are structured, that the requirements of those needs are such that they enjoin the manner in which they must be satisfied if the organism is to function as a healthy whole. Indeed, it will be shown that the facts of man's biological nature, what *is,* determine the direction his development as a person must take. That is to say, that what *is* here clearly determines what *ought to be;* in short, that the biological facts give a biological validation to the principle of cooperation, or love, in human life. In other words, we can here demonstrate that there are certain values for human life which are not matters of opinion but which are biologically determined. If we do violence to those inbuilt values, we disorder our lives, as persons, as groups, as nations, and as a world of human beings whose biological drives are directed toward love, toward cooperation. If we can clearly grasp the meaning of the facts, and they are easily understood, we shall the more readily be in a position to put them to practical use. Let us to the facts, then.

THE FIRST STEP

THE INFANT, AT BIRTH, IS EQUIPPED WITH active drives to receive love from the mother. Here the first fulfillment of these drives is a fundamental cooperative act. As Alfred Adler has pointed out, "the first act of a new-born child—drinking from the mother's breast—is cooperation, and is as pleasant for the mother as for the child." [30] There is the tactile stimulation about the lips and face, the tongue, the oral cavity, and the liquid stimulation of the gastrointestinal tract. Here, in this act, is the first step in the development of the sense of contact with another person. In Adler's words:

---

[30] A. Adler, *Social Interest: A Challenge to Mankind*, Putnam, New York, 1938, p. 214.

. . . the child's inclination to cooperation is challenged from the very first day. The immense importance of the mother in this respect can be clearly recognized. She stands on the threshold of the development of social feeling. The biological heritage of social feeling is entrusted to her charge. She can strengthen or hinder contact by the help she gives the child in little things, in bathing him, in providing all that a helpless infant is in need of. Her relations with the child, her knowledge, and her aptitude are decisive factors. . . . It may readily be accepted that contact with the mother is of the highest importance for the development of human social feeling. . . . *We probably owe to the maternal sense of contact the largest part of human social feeling, and along with it the essential continuance of human civilization.*[31]

Frustration of the drives to receive love from the mother (not necessarily the biological mother, a mother surrogate will do) at this period not only produces anxiety in the infant but also a retention of unexpressed hunger for tangible mother love, which may then find an outlet through gastrointestinal disease. Similarly, if the infant's cries for attention remain unanswered, the unsatisfied tensions may express themselves through the bronchial tree in the form of asthma.[32] Such responses constitute involuntary emergency discharges through the organ systems involved in the frustration of the need. The energies which should have been discharged outward are now discharged inward.[33] The affection of the organ or organ systems becomes a substitute affect-equivalent for the original gratification sought by the organism. A large proportion of, if not all, neuroses and psychosomatic disorders may be so explained, their

---

[31] *Ibid.*, pp. 220–21.

[32] F. Alexander, "Psychogenic Factors in Bronchial Asthma," Part I, *Psychosomatic Medicine*, IV, 1941, p. 58.

[33] For a discussion of the organ neuroses, see O. Fenichel, *The Psychoanalytic Theory of the Neuroses*, Norton, New York, 1945, pp. 236–267.

foundations being laid within the first six years of life.

The importance of love in the early social development of the infant cannot be overemphasized. Its real significance can best be understood when we consider a disease from which, but half a century ago, almost all the children hospitalized within their first year of life regularly died.[34] This disease was known as marasmus, from the Greek word meaning "wasting away." The disease was also known as infantile atrophy or debility; today it is known as "hospitalism."[35] When intensive studies were undertaken to track down its cause, the discovery was made that babies in the best homes and hospitals were most often its victims, babies who were apparently receiving the best and most careful physical attention, while babies in the poorest homes, with a

[34] In a report on ten different cities in the United States, Dr. Henry Chapin, in 1915, found that in all but one institution every infant under two years of age died (H. D. Chapin, "A Plea for Accurate Statistics in Infants' Institutions," *Transactions of the American Pediatric Society*, vol. 27, 1915, p. 180). The various discussants of Dr. Chapin's paper fully corroborated his findings from their own experience. Dr. R. Hamil remarking with grim irony "I had the honor to be connected with an institution in this city [Philadelphia] in which the mortality among all the infants under one year of age, when admitted to the institution and retained there for any length of time, was 100 per cent." Dr. R. T. Southworth added, "I can give an instance from an institution [in New York City] that no longer exists in which, on account of the very considerable mortality among the infants admitted, it was customary to enter the condition of every infant on the admission card as hopeless. That covered all subsequent happenings." Finally, Dr. J. H. M. Knox described a study which he had made in Baltimore. Of 200 infants admitted to various institutions almost 90 per cent died within a year. The 10 per cent that survived, he stated, did so apparently because they were taken from the institutions for short times and placed in the care of foster parents or relatives.

[35] For the recommended changes in the management of hospitalized children see J. R. Robertson, *Young Children in Hospital*, Tavistock Publications, London, 1958.

good mother, despite the lack of hygienic physical conditions, often overcame the physical handicaps and flourished. What was wanting in the sterilized environment of the babies of the first category and was generously supplied in babies of the second category was mother love.

This discovery is responsible for the fact that most hospitals today endeavor to keep the infant for as short a period as possible. The best place for the infant is with its mother, and, if its own mother is not available, with a foster mother, for what the infant must have is love. Drs. Ruth and Harry Bakwin, pediatricians of great experience, point out that:

The effect of residence in a hospital manifests itself by a fairly well-defined clinical picture. A striking feature is the failure to gain properly, despite the ingestion of diets which are entirely adequate for growth in the home. Infants in hospitals sleep less than others and they rarely smile or babble spontaneously. They are listless and apathetic and look unhappy. The appetite is indifferent and food is accepted without enthusiasm. The stools tend to be frequent and, in sharp contrast with infants cared for in the home, it is unusual for 24 hours to pass without an evacuation. Respiratory infections which last only a day or two in the home are prolonged and may persist for weeks or months. Return to the home results in defervescence (disappearance of fever) within a few days and a prompt and striking gain in weight.[36]

The emotional deprivation suffered by infants in hospitals may do vastly more damage than the physical condition which brought them there.[37] The infant can

---

[36] Ruth M. Bakwin and Harry Bakwin, *Psychologic Care During Infancy and Childhood*, Appleton-Century Co., New York, 1942, p. 295.

[37] For a particularly poignant and not untypical case see D. MacCarthy and R. MacKeith, "A Parent's Voice," *The Lancet* (*ii*) December 18, 1965, pp. 1289–1291, and the correspondence in subsequent issues.

suffer no greater loss than the privation of its mother's love, for it would seem that the satisfaction of the generalized feeling of dependency, in itself a basic need, is best accomplished through mother love. Because the mother is the person usually most profoundly interested in the welfare of her infant, it is from her that the infant receives the supports and reassurances which love bestows. This is not to say that some other person not the mother of the infant could not do as much for it. There is good reason to believe that devoted foster mothers or nurses have often successfully taken the place of the actual mother in giving the infant all the love it required. At Bellevue Hospital, in New York, it has become "the custom to assign infants who are doing poorly or who seem unhappy" to particular interns for "tender loving care." "This device," remarks Dr. Harry Bakwin, "has been well received in most instances and it has often proved as beneficial for the intern as for the baby." [38]

The relationship between hospitalism and absence of mothering is proven by two types of facts. The first is the rapidity with which the symptoms disappear as soon as the baby is given a sufficient amount of love either in or outside the hospital, and the second is the fact that hospitalism or institutionalism does not occur in hospitals in which each child receives an adequate amount of love. Normally, however, the infant receives its love from the person best qualified to give it, the biological mother.

Now let us see what is likely to happen to the infant who is deprived of his mother shortly after birth. An illuminating example is the following case, described by Dr. Margaret Ribble:

---

[38] H. Bakwin, "Emotional Depression in Infants," *Journal of Pediatrics*, vol. 35, 1949, p. 520.

Little Bob was born in the maternity hospital where the writer was making studies of infants at the time. He was a full-term child and weighed six pounds three ounces at birth. During the two weeks' stay in the hospital the baby was breast-fed and there was no apparent difficulty with his body functions. The mother, a professional woman, had been reluctant about breast-feeding because she wished to take up her work as soon as possible after the baby was born, but she yielded to the kindly encouragement of the hospital nurses, and the feeding was successful. Both mother and child were thriving when they left the hospital.

On returning home, the mother found that her husband had suddenly deserted her—the climax of an unhappy and maladjusted marriage relationship. She discovered soon after that her milk did not agree with the baby. As is frequently the case, the deep emotional reaction had affected her milk secretion. The infant refused the breast and began to vomit. Later he was taken to the hospital and the mother did not call to see him. At the end of a month she wrote that she had been seriously ill and asked the hospital to keep the child until further notice.

In spite of careful medical attention and skillful feeding, this baby remained for two months at practically the same weight. He was in a crowded ward and received very little personal attention. The busy nurses had no time to mother him and play with him as a mother would, or to change his position and make him comfortable at frequent intervals. The habit of finger-sucking developed, and gradually the child became what is known as a ruminator, his food coming up and going down with equal ease. At the age of two months he weighed five pounds. The baby at this time was transferred to a small children's hospital, with the idea that this institution might be able to give him more individual care. It became apparent that the mother had abandoned the child altogether.

When seen by the writer, this baby actually looked like a seven months' foetus, yet he had also a strange appearance of oldness. His arms and legs were wrinkled and wasted, his head large in proportion to the rest of his body, his chest round and flaring wildly at the base over an enormous liver. His breathing was shallow, he was generally inactive, and his skin was cold and flabby. He took large quanties of milk, but did not gain weight since most of it went through him with very little assimilation and with copious discharges of mucus from his intestines. The baby showed at this time the pallor which, in our study, we have found typical of infants who are not mothered.

There was no definite evidence of organic disease, but growth and development were definitely at a standstill, and it appeared that the child was gradually slipping backward to prenatal levels of body economy and function.

The routine treatment at the new hospital for the baby who is not gaining weight is to give him concentrated nursing care. He is held by the nurse for all feedings and allowed at least half an hour to take the bottle. From time to time his position in the crib is changed, and, when possible, the nurse carries him about the ward for a few minutes before or after each feeding. This is the closest possible approach to mothering in a busy infants' ward. Medical treatment consists of frequent injections of salt solution under the skin to support the weakened circulation in the surface of the body and prevent dehydration.

With this treatment, little Bob began to improve slowly. As his physical condition became better, it was possible for our research group to introduce the services of a volunteer "mother," who came to the hospital twice daily in order to give him some of the attention he so greatly needed. What she actually did was to hold him in her lap for a short period before feedings. She was told that he needed love more than he needed medicine, and she was instructed to stroke the child's head gently and speak or sing softly to him and walk him about. Her daily visits were gradually prolonged until she was spending an hour twice a day, giving the baby this artificial mothering. The result was good. The child remained in the hospital until he was five months of age, at which time he weighed nine pounds. All rumination and diarrhea had stopped, and he had become an alert baby with vigorous muscular activity. His motor coordinations were, of course, retarded. Although he held up his head well and looked about, focusing his eyes and smiling in response to his familiar nurses, he could not yet grasp his bottle or turn himself over, as is customary at this age. The finger-sucking continued, as is usually the case with babies who have suffered early privation.

In accordance with the new hospital procedure, as soon as the child's life was no longer in danger, he was transferred to a good, supervised foster home in order that he might have still more individual attention. Under this regime, his development proceeded well and gradually he mastered such functions as sitting, creeping, and standing. His speech was slow in developing, however, and he did not walk until after the second year. The general health of this child was excellent at the end of his third year; also his I.Q. was high on standard tests, but his emotional life was deeply damaged. With any change in his routine or with a prolonged absence of the foster mother, he would go into a state quite similar to a depression. He became inactive, ate very little, had intestinal disturbances and was extremely pale. When his foster mother was away, he usually reacted with a loss of body tone and alertness, rather than with a definite protest. His emotional relationship to the foster mother was receptive, like that of a young infant, but he made little response to her mothering activities except to function better when she was there. He had little capacity to express affection, displayed no initiative in seeking it, yet failed to thrive without it. This lack of response made it difficult for the foster mother to show him the consistent love which he so deeply needed. Without the frequent explanations of the situation from the visiting nurse, she would probably have given up the care of the child.[39]

Evidence gathered by many investigators renders it highly probable that to a greater or lesser extent the history of the emotional development of this child represents the history of most unmothered infants.[40] The history of this child is by no means extreme, but it does illustrate, rather strikingly, the effects upon the newborn and infant of the absence of the stimulus which a mother's love or that of a mother surrogate provides. Without that stimulus, the psychosomatic effects upon the child are often disastrous. Such a child may be emotionally crippled for life. As adults, such children remain fixated at their early dependent, infantile level, they demand affection but cannot easily return it.

Studies carried out on children who have spent their infancy in institutions lead to the conclusion, in Lowrey's words, that such infants

---

[39] Margaret Ribble, *The Rights of Infants*, 2nd ed., Columbia University Press, New York, 1965, pp. 5–9.

[40] John Bowlby, *Maternal Care and Mental Health*, WHO Publications, Columbia University Press, New York, 1951; M. D. Ainsworth *et al.*, *Deprivation of Maternal Care*, WHO Publications, Columbia University Press, New York, 1962; L. Casler, *Maternal Deprivation: A Critical Review of the Literature*, Monographs of the Society for Research in Child Growth and Development, vol. 26, no. 2, 1961; R. G. Patton and L. I. Gardner, *Growth Failure and Maternal Deprivation*, Thomas, Springfield, Illinois, 1963.

undergo an isolation type of experience with resulting isolation type of personality, characterized by unsocial behavior, hostile aggression, lack of patterns for giving and receiving affection, inability to understand and accept limitations, much insecurity in adapting to environment. These children present delays in development and intensification as well as prolongation of behavior manifestations at these levels. At the time of transfer (to a foster home), the children are at a stage when they can form only partial love attachments; hostility and aggression are at a peak; egocentricity is marked, and they do not recognize the individuality and needs of others. They are unprepared for and unequal to the demands and limitations of a family setting. They are exposed to attention and affection far in excess of anything they have previously known, and react excessively either by extravagant behavior, negativism or both.[41]

The work of Goldfarb and of many other investigators has demonstrated conclusively that the institutionally reared child is characterized by a personality which is strikingly less differentiated than that of the home-reared loved child. Such children are markedly more passive and apathetic as a consequence, presumably, of their highly routinized experience. Motivation and ambition is lacking. Language retardation is severe and persists well into adolescence. Aggressive behavior and instability of emotional response is usual, and deficiencies of inhibition the rule. They are restless, aimless in their behavior, unreflective, and lacking in persistence. The impoverished social environment of the institution, the lack of a dynamic and varied social experience, is reflected in the inability of the institutionalized child to develop meaningful reciprocal human relationships. The lack of loving attention, affection, and stimulation of the family, with its human protecting and supporting ties, in the experience of such children, leads to a marked

---

[41] Lawson G. Lowrey, "Personality Distortion and Early Institutional Care," *American Journal of Orthopsychiatry*, vol. 10, 1935, pp. 576–85.

insecurity with a resulting hunger for attention and affection. In the younger children attention-seeking behavior is particularly marked, and this is usually combined with hostile, overtly aggressive acts. Eventually, the conflict between the need for affection and the inability to respond to normal human relationships is resolved by a more consistent defense of emotional isolation, resulting in apathetic social responses and a pattern of withdrawal from life's tasks.[42]

Such children, while they may improve following adoption into a family, seldom recover from the effects of their early deprivations. It is not difficult to recognize such persons in adulthood. The basic personality defects are congealed at a level of extreme immaturity. By the age of six years, the damage has been effectively done that will mar the institution child for the rest of his life.

As Goldfarb points out, "Under normal circumstances, early dependency becomes the constructive basis for the development of a growing and secure sense of independence. In other words, independence is a positive and mature adaptation based on secure grasp of the self

---

[42] For the best account of research findings on the personality of the institutionalized child, see William Goldfarb, "The Effects of Early Institutional Care on Adolescent Personality," *Journal of Experimental Education*, vol. 12, 1943, pp. 106–129; also the following papers by the same author, "Infant Rearing and Problem Behavior," *American Journal of Orthopsychiatry*, vol. 13, 1943, pp. 249–265; "The Effects of Early Institutional Care on Adolescent Personality (Graphic Rorschach Data)," *Child Development*, vol. 14, 1943, pp. 213–223; "Infant Rearing as a Factor in Foster Home Replacement," *American Journal of Orthopsychiatry*, vol. 14, 1944, pp. 162–166; "Psychological Privation in Infancy and Subsequent Adjustment," *American Journal of Orthopsychiatry*, vol. 15, 1945, pp. 247–255; "Effects of Psychological Deprivation in Infancy and Subsequent Stimulation," *American Journal of Psychiatry*, vol. 102, 1945, pp. 18–33. For a discussion of these and similar studies see Ashley Montagu, *The Direction of Human Development*, Harper, New York, 1955.

in relation to other people. This is to be differentiated from the isolation reaction of the institution group, for the latter reaction represents defensive adaptation to a confused, hazy, and thus fearful grasp of one's relationship to the world of people and things as well as to inadequate methods for meeting reality." [43]

The dependency needs normally satisfied by the mother are in institution children *inadequately* satisfied, and the result is a more or less permanent failure of development of the affective life of the person.

It is important to note that *inadequate* satisfaction of the dependency needs, *not* complete deprivation, is sufficient to produce this failure of affective development. It appears that the damage done is related to the degree of privation suffered by the infant. For example, rejected children will show similar symptoms to institution children. The differences, however, are very significant, varying with the conditions.

The deprivation situation is characterized by · a marked poverty of affective and social stimulation. In the institution child this is further reinforced by the handicapping barrenness and narrowness of the institution environment. The world of things and of people, of experience as something lived or undergone, is flattened out and severely limited. The interstimulation of family relationships in all their manifold aspects is lost. And as Goldfarb so well puts it, "The institution child thus establishes no specific identifications and engages in no meaningful reciprocal relationships with the people. The basic motivations to normal maturation and differentiation of personality are absent. Paucity in content and organization of both intellect and feeling follow. The ego structure is primitive and undeveloped. . . .

---

[43] William Goldfarb, *op. cit.,* p. 128.

Both the 'I' of the inner life, and the 'It' of the outer life, are crippled."[44]

On the other hand, while the rejected child may suffer from a greater or lesser degree of affective deprivation, the horizon of its experience is usually nowhere nearly as limited as that of the institution child. Hence, the rejected child does not usually exhibit any defects in abstract thinking as does the institution child; his span of attention and his concentrative powers are not as crippled. He is more anxious, more ambitiously purposeful, and has a much greater capacity for insight. He therefore usually responds to treatment, whereas the institution child rarely responds effectively.

In some homes the rejection of the child has been so extreme as to produce symptoms in it of deprivation identical with those of the institution child.[45] This is an area of social pathology which requires continuous investigation and attention.

So far as the effects of varying forms of privation upon the personality are concerned, the evidence now available for nonliterate and other peoples is extremely suggestive.

In Western societies there are great variations in the kind and amount of mothering which infants receive. Class differences here play an important role. Among the upper classes the mother tends to shift the burden of "mothering" the infant to a nurse as soon as possible. In Europe and, until very recently, in the South, upper-class children were almost always brought up by nurses and governesses. In the middle classes, the mother tended to care for her own child a good deal of the time,

---

[44] William Goldfarb, "Psychological Privation in Infancy and Subsequent Adjustment," *op. cit.*, p. 254.

[45] R. G. Patton and L. I. Gardner, *Growth Failure and Maternal Deprivation*, Thomas, Springfield, Illinois, 1963.

at least during the newborn and infancy periods, even though a nurse or governess was also employed. Among the lower classes universally the mother is the person who gives the child most attention. To what extent these differences in "mothering" affect the development of personality is a matter for future research to determine. It is possible that such differences in "mothering" in the early months and years of life will be found to have a profound effect on character.[46]

In this particular field we need more research studies. It will not be enough to inquire into the personality development of unmothered children, though this is indispensable. It is also highly desirable to discover the variation in the quality of mothering which different mothers have given their children, and to inquire into the exact amount and quality of mothering the person has received from the mother and how much from nurses and other persons.

The upper-class Englishman (and Englishwoman) may prove to be good material for the investigation of this problem. Over and beyond the fact that the early training and inhibitions of the upper-class Englishman prevent him from ever exhibiting much emotion, there is detectable a certain lack of warmth which, in common with the members of the upper classes of other nations, may be found to be due to an early lack of mothering. Not all members of the upper classes exhibit this lack of warmth and many members of the middle and lower classes may show it. This lack of warmth in adults often signifies the inability to love other persons, and in such adults one usually looks in vain for that

---

[46] Sylvia Brody, *Patterns of Mothering*, International Universities Press, New York, 1956. B. M. Spinley, *The Deprived and the Privileged*, Routledge, London, 1953.

human sympathy with others which one finds in those who have been adequately loved. It may seem a bit far-fetched to suggest that the ability of the upper-middle- and upper-class Englishman to rule and govern subject peoples and to justify that rule, has, in the past at least, to some extent been due to such lack of sympathetic understanding for others.[47]

The custom among the upper and upper-middle classes in England of sending their children away to boarding schools at an early age, of institutionalizing them, as it were, outside the warm ambience of the family, deprives these children of the love and affection which is necessary for the healthy development of the personality. This privation of parental love suffered during the tender years of childhood is probably one of the causes of the apparent "coldness," the seemingly unemotional character of the upper-class Englishman. On this aspect of the Englishman's character, E. M. Forster has an interesting passage:

People talk of the mysterious East, but the West also is mysterious. It has depths that do not reveal themselves at the first glance. We know what the sea looks like from a distance; it is of one color, and level, and obviously cannot contain such creatures as fish. But if we look into the sea over the edge of a boat, we see a dozen colors, and depth below depth, and fish swimming in them. That sea is the English character—apparently imperturbable and even. The depths and the colors are the English romanticism and the English sensitiveness—we do not expect to find such things, but they exist. And—to continue my metaphor—the fish are the English emotions, which are always trying to get up to the surface, but don't quite know how. For the most part we see them moving far below, distorted and ob-

---

[47] For some interesting comments bearing upon these points, see Geoffrey Gorer, "Some Notes on the British Character," *Horizon*, vol. 20, 1949/50, pp. 369–379. See also the same author's *Exploring English Character*, New York, Criterion Books, 1955.

scure. Now and then they succeed and we exclaim, "Why, the Englishman has emotions! He actually can feel!" And occasionally we see that beautiful creature, the flying fish, which rises out of the water altogether into the air and sunlight. English literature is a flying fish. It is a sample of the life that goes on day after day beneath the surface; it is a proof that beauty and emotion exist in the salt, inhospitable sea.[48]

Quite in contrast to the Englishman's emotional restraint is the emotional warmth and sensitivity of, say, the Italian [49] or the Russian.[50] It is significant that the Italian or Russian family is one in which the members are closely bound to one another in a loving, emotional atmosphere which is very different from that found among English-speaking peoples. In pre-Communist Russia it was very generally considered a tragedy for a Russian girl to entertain the idea of marrying an Englishman—"cold fish" apparently utterly inacapable of all emotion! The Italians still entertain similar views concerning the English—not altogether unjustifiably.

---

[48] E. M. Forster, *Abinger Harvest*, Harcourt, Brace, New York, 1947. For a beautiful exemplification of the type, see Timothy Eden, *The Tribulations of a Baronet*, Macmillan, London, 1933; see also R. Hart-Davis, *Hugh Walpole: A Biography*, Macmillan, New York, 1952.

[49] For the Italians see J. H. Burns, *The Gallery*, Harper, New York, 1948; H. Kubly, *An American in Italy*, Simon & Schuster, New York, 1955; Luigi Barzini, *The Italians*, Atheneum, New York, 1964.

[50] For the Russians see P. Sorokin, *Russia and the United States*, New York, 1944; George Brandes, *Impressions of Russia*, Scribner's, New York, 1890.

NO MAN IS AN ISLAND

IN ALL THE EXAMPLES OF FAILURE OF ONE kind or another in the course of mothering, of satisfaction of basic needs, we perceive as the end effect the failure to develop social competence, for social interaction is simply the extension of mother-child interaction, and the ability of the person to interact socially will depend largely upon the character of his early interaction with his mother or mother-surrogate.

To telescope much into a few words, as the child matures and the socialization process continues, with its frustrations as well as its satisfactions, the child becomes more and more firmly bound to the socializing agent, more and more dependent rather than more free, and this social binding continues throughout life. This view of the development of the person cannot be too strongly emphasized. Its implications are of the first order of importance. The conventional view of the person in the socializing process as developing to greater and greater individuality is a seriously misleading one. Of course, everyone has a unique personality in the sense that it is never identical with that of any other person, and the differences between personalities are important and tend to become more distinct with age. This is something to be thankful for. But it must be realized that every one of these differences has developed under the influence of socializing factors, and that were it not for the creative action of those socializing factors, the functional-structural differences which characterize each person would not be as great as they are. Every person is socially bound to the group in which he has been socialized. In this sense the "individual" is a myth. From the standpoint of the social situation there are no individuals, except as abstracted biological entities or for the quantitative purposes of a census. Even from the physical and physiological standpoints, it is doubtful whether the individual has a separate existence in any but an arbitrary sense. Are we not, in the term "individual," creating separateness where separateness does not, in fact, exist? Certainly individualization in man exceeds that attained by any other animal, but it is an individualization which takes place more fully in relation to the group than it does in any other living creature. A creature apart from a social group is nothing but an organic being. The member of a social group is a person, a personality developed under the molding influence of social interstimulation. The person is a set of social relationships. As Bogardus has put it, "As a result of intersocial stimulation, he moves up from the biological level. The interstimulation that occurs between him and members of the group, not as mere individuals but as persons, explains him more than any other method of approach can do." [51]

The "rugged American individualist," for example, is no more an individualist than is a soldier sniping at the enemy. Both behave as they do because they have been subordinated to imperatives which in each case are functions of their social conditioning. They act as they do because they are the results of certain historically conditioned social processes. They act as they do not because they are independent individuals, but because they are dependent persons bound to their social group and must maintain their relationships in that group in the manner, in each case, allowed and encouraged by the group.

Free will the individual certainly has in the sense of the ability to achieve purposes, and with a certain element of novelty, that is, of causal unrelatedness. But for all its varied and important possibilities for spontaneity and novelty it is a will that acts strictly within the limits of the pattern determined by the social group. The spontaneous conduct of the person is still conduct based on models established in a particular social group. In short, the person is an interdependent system of social relationships which may by abstraction alone be recognized as a unit.

It cannot be too strongly emphasized that this view of the relationship of man to his fellow men in society does not mean that the social process makes automata out of men. Even in the most totalitarian of states, Nazi Germany, men had not yet been turned into machines, and however much like automata they may have ap-

---

[51] Emory S. Bogardus, (Discussion) in Floyd H. Allport, "The Group Fallacy in Relation to Social Science," *American Journal of Sociology,* vol. 29, 1924, p. 704.

peared, they were far from being so; they were still human beings, however much misguided. And that is the point. It is possible to mislead human beings, and human beings are constantly in danger of being so deceived. The danger is such that it would, in fact, be possible to transform human beings into at least reasonable facsimiles of automata.[52] In virtue of the fact that man is behaviorally so malleable a creature he can be molded to almost any possible behavioral form. Because this is so, because of the danger of "insectification," as someone has termed it, of mankind, we must make quite certain that there is nothing in our ideas or conduct which might lead to the debasement of man. More positively, we must recognize what it is that requires to be done. To understand that men are inextricably bound to each other, and that the will which they have as persons because it acts strictly within the limits determined by the pattern of the social group constitutes reason for alarm as well as for hope. Alarm, because man is capable of extreme and fatal confusions, and must therefore be constantly on guard against these, and hope because he is equally capable of discovering truths which can teach him to live in fruitful and creative harmony with himself and his fellow men. This alarm may be recognized as vigilance, but is more accurately described by the term anxiety. A certain amount of anxiety accompanies the expression of all needs,[53] and when these needs are perceived as the

---

[52] What could be done this way and how has been the theme of several novels, Aldous Huxley, *Brave New World*, Harper, New York, 1931; George Orwell, *1984*, Harcourt, Brace, New York, 1948; Ray Bradbury, *Fahrenheit 451*, Ballantine Books, New York, 1953.

[53] Lawrence S. Kubie, "Instincts and Homeostasis," *Psychosomatic Medicine*, X, 1948, pp. 15–30.

total functioning of the organism, they are seen to constitute the one great need: the need to be loved *and* to love others.

It is necessary to be anxious, to be vigilant, concerning one's needs, and the manner in which they are to be satisfied. But this does not mean that one has to be constantly worrying about them, anymore than one needs to worry about being dry in order to satisfy one's need for water. It does, however, mean that one must be alert to all possible changes in the environment, for the environment is part of ourselves, as we are part of it. Finally, it means that it is imperatively important for man to discover the requirements which must be fulfilled if he is to live in harmony with himself and his fellow men—with his total environment. It should always be remembered that separation between the organism and its environment is, again, an arbitrary act. As Leo Loeb put it in a masterly work, "In consequence of the more and more intricate interaction between environment and psychical-social individuality, a separation between individuality and environment, especially the social environment, becomes impossible." [54]

And that is the truth which should forever shatter what we must insist on calling the pathetic fallacy, the organismal fallacy that man is essentially a function of his genes. The biologically exclusive sacredness of the individual is a chimera not only as regards man but as regards all other animal groups. The biologist of an earlier day may have cried "The individual for itself." To this the great physiologist Sir Charles Sherrington has made the proper reply:

The individual? What are the most successful individuals which

---

[54] Leo Loeb, *The Biological Basis of Individuality,* Thomas, Springfield, Illinois, 1944, pp. 651–652.

Life has to show? The multi-cellular. And what has gone to their making? The multi-cellular organism is in itself a variant from the perennial antagonism of cell and cell. Instead of that eternal antagonism, it is a making use of relatedness to bind cell to cell for cooperation. The multi-cellular organism stood for a change, in so far, from conflict between cell and cell to harmony between cell and cell. Its coming was, we know now, pregnant with an immense advance for the whole future of life upon the globe. It was potential of the present success of living forms upon the planet. Implicit in it was for one thing, the emergence of recognizable mind. It was among the many-celled organisms that recognizable mind first appeared. It is surely more than mere analogy to liken to those small beginnings of multi-cellular life of millions of years ago the slender beginnings of altruism today. Evolution has constantly dealt with the relation between physical and mental as more than mere analogy. The bond of cohesion now arising instead of being as then one of material contact and interchange between related cell-lives is in its nature mental. It is a projection of the self by sympathy with other life into organismal situations besides its immediate own. It is altruism as passion. It marks, we may think, at the present time the climax of mind.[55]

To bind cell to cell for cooperation, that is the essence of social life. But no cell is more intricately bound to another than is man to his fellows and his social group. The binding of the individual to his group represents, in fact, a loss of *individual* freedom and a gain in *personal* development through more or less complete identification with the social group. An identification in which the wholeness of the person is preserved only because it is a functioning part of a greater whole—society.

In this process the consciousness of self may actually increase, the sense of personal identity may become even more vivid, and one's ties to one's society more firmly established than ever. Individuation, as the development of personal identity, is neither the contrary

[55] Charles Sherrington, *Man on His Nature*, Cambridge University Press, 1941, pp. 387–388.

nor the contradictory of social identification; it *is* social identification.[56]

The individual—the set of physical and physiological functions—becomes a person with a definite identity only through the process of socialization—the process of becoming identified with a social group. Dissociations such as are implied in the phrases "the self in conflict with society," "man against society" imply a false separation of conditions. Society is made up of interacting selves, of men. It *is* men in interaction. The conditions of conflict which arise in man do not normally originate from within him, from his organic states, but from those social conditions which have a disordering effect upon him and which fail to satisfy his needs. In this sense a neurosis may be produced as the result of a disorder of some part of his social experience to which the person has been unable to adjust himself.

The importance of institutions in determining the nature of neuroses is most clearly seen in those cases in which the structure of the culture is such as to omit any institutionalization of certain forms of behavior. Here, neuroses of certain kinds never occur, whereas in cultures presenting such institutionalized forms of behavior, neurotic forms of behavior with specific reference to these institutions do occur. For example, shamanism and possession are forms of behavior which occur wherever beliefs in the supernatural and the ability of supernatural powers to take possession of certain persons are strongly held.[57] Where such beliefs do not exist or are weakly developed, shamanism does not oc-

---

[56] See the writings of Erik H. Erikson, especially *Childhood and Society*, 2nd ed., Norton, New York, 1963, and *Insight and Responsibility*, Norton, New York, 1964.

[57] Mircea Eliade, *Shamanism: Archaic Techniques of Ecstasy*, Pantheon Books, New York, 1964.

cur. In medieval Europe, when such beliefs were the rule, witchcraft and possession were common phenomena. With the decline in the belief in the supernatural, witches and possession have all but disappeared in Europe—to be replaced by a counterpart which fits more satisfactorily into the existing cultural structure: the witchcraft and neurosis of modern times known as racism.[58]

Persons, that is, socialized individuals, come into being only through social interactions. "They are differentiations within the social field of relations. The group, therefore, is genetically prior to personality." [59]

The identity of the person consists of and is derived from the meaningfulness of his interrelationships.

In short, the physiological dependency of the fetus and the newborn becomes, in society, a socially organized dependency, a social dependency in which the interacting person finds the meaning of his life in his relations with other persons and their thoughts and activities. Unheeded, the physiologically dependent infant would die. Unheeded, the socially dependent adult falls into an apathy which may lead to death. As Erich Fromm has put it, "Unless the person feels that he belongs somewhere, unless his life has some meaning and direction, he would feel like a particle of dust and be overcome by his individual insignificance. He would not be able to relate himself to any system which would give meaning and direction to his life, he would be filled with doubt and this doubt eventually would paralyze his ability to act—that is, to live." [60]

[58] Ashley Montagu, *Man's Most Dangerous Myth: The Fallacy of Race*, 4th ed., World Publishing Co., Cleveland, 1964.

[59] John E. Boodin, *The Social Mind*, Macmillan, New York, 1939, p. 155.

[60] Erich Fromm, *Escape from Freedom*, Farrar & Rinehart, New York, 1941, pp. 21–22.

Now, as John Fiske has originally pointed out, and many others since, the long period of dependency which is characteristic of the human infant generates social conditions leading to the peculiar developments of human culture. The importance of this lengthy period of dependence cannot be overemphasized,[61] but the emphasis can be, and often has been, wrongly placed.[62] Were the anthropoid apes characterized by a period of dependent infancy ten times as long as man's, they would still not develop anything resembling human culture, since they do not possess the necessary genetic potentialities. Failing these, the length of the infant dependency period has a very limited significance for the development of culture, but once granted such potentialities, the length of the dependency period becomes of major significance, and what we know as peculiarly human society is inevitable.

This is not to say that were the human infant so constructed as to be able to learn to walk, think, talk, and care for himself within a few weeks after birth, human culture would not have developed. It would most certainly have done so, but it is equally certain that the human personality would be an appreciably different thing from what it is today. It is also very likely that societies would be very much more atomistically constructed than they are today. However this may be, the fact is that the prolonged period of infant dependency produces interactive behavior of a kind which within

---

[61] For the evidence indicating that at birth the human infant has still to complete its gestation outside the womb see Ashley Montagu, *The Human Revolution*, World Publishing Co., Cleveland, 1965, pp. 122–131.

[62] For an example of this see Geza Roheim's interesting work, *The Origin and Function of Culture*, Nervous and Mental Disease Monographs, New York, No. 69, 1943.

the first six years of the child's life determines the primary pattern of his subsequent social development.

As we have pointed out, it is within this period that he learns to love others: the mother who has so consistently, intimately, and lovingly attended to his needs; the father, his brothers and sisters, and whoever else has participated in the process of satisfying his needs. Certain persons become to him the symbols of satisfaction, for they are always the objects which provide him with the means of satisfaction, and the first conditioning which the child undergoes is this: that persons who have fairly consistently provided the infant with the means of satisfying its needs now become satisfying objects in themselves. The satisfaction of its basic needs becomes indissolubly associated in the infant's mind with persons who have provided those satisfactions.

The mother is, of course, normally the principal producer of satisfactions and she becomes the first love-object of the child. In this sequence of events, from prenatal to postnatal life, can be seen the determinants, as it were, in high relief, of the pattern of life which every person everywhere seeks to secure, namely, a state of dependency in which one's needs are satisfied by persons whom one (therefore) loves.

What human beings desire most of all is to have their needs satisfied, to be made secure. They also want to feel dependent, either upon some mother-ideal, deity, or other persons, or, pathologically, narcissistically upon themselves, but dependent they must feel. Man does not want to be independent, free, in the sense of functioning independently of the interests of his fellows. This kind of negative independence leads to lonesomeness, isolation, and fear.[63] What man wants is that positive

[63] Margaret M. Wood, *Paths of Loneliness*, Columbia University Press, New York, 1953.

freedom which follows the pattern of his life as an infant within the family—dependent security, the feeling that one is a part of a group, accepted, wanted, loved, and loving.

The directiveness and creativeness of the human organism at birth is toward realization in terms of dependency upon other organisms. Everything we know points to this fact.

John Donne beautifully expressed these ideas in his seventeenth "Devotion":

No man is an *Island,* entire of itself; every man is a piece of the *Continent,* a part of the *main;* if a *Clod* be washed away by the *Sea, Europe* is the less, as well as if a *Promontory* were, as well as if a *Manor* of thy *friends* or of thine *own* were; any man's *death* diminishes *me,* because I am involved in *Mankind;* And therefore never send to know for whom the *bell* tolls; it tolls for thee.

Because I am involved in mankind. That, in brief, is the whole story, for no man can ever be other than involved in mankind. Human beings by their very nature are involved with and dependent upon other human beings all the days of their lives.

The phenomenon of transference as seen in the psychoanalytic situation constitutes, as Freud has pointed out, a proof that adults do not overcome their childhood dependency.[64] In the transference situation, the patient develops relations toward the therapist which are clearly derived from emotions originally directed toward the parents. The feelings of dependency upon the parents are transferred to the therapist. The patient becomes deeply attached to his analyst, he falls in love with him, overestimates his qualities, will not tolerate a word said against him, and does everything in his

---

[64] Sigmund Freud, "Psychoanalysis," *Encyclopaedia Britannica,* 14th Edition, 1929, pp. 672–674.

power to maintain the dependent relationship. What he is doing, in fact, is to reproduce the dependency situation of his early infancy. The transference relationship is utilized by the therapist to make this clear to the patient and is thus converted into an instrument for his re-education.

A person is not an object in itself, except for census purposes, but a function of activities which he exhibits in interaction with other persons, that is to say, the constituent interacting element of culture. As Harry Stack Sullivan has suggested, personality "is the hypothetical entity that one postulates to account for the doings of people, one with another, and with more or less personified objects." [65] Personality is, in fact, an abstraction, the segmentation of a process at a particular time involving the behavior of a person in relation to others. Whether it is the ego that is doing the segmenting or judging of other persons, the personality is always a function of relations with other persons. The person is a set of interpersonal relationships, and it is during infancy that the pattern which these shall take is largely determined.

Love is an active state which is learned by the infant, and it is a state which is developed in interdependency, and that is the pattern of love which is maintained throughout the life of the person. We love only those things to which we feel ourselves bound—not, however, all things to which we feel related: those which are associated with frustration we hate, but those which are associated with pleasure, either present, recollected or anticipated, we love.

Man is related to himself only in so far as he is related

---

[65] Harry S. Sullivan, "Psychiatry: Introduction to the Study of Interpersonal Relations," *Psychiatry*, vol. 1, 1938, pp. 121–134.

to others. To love is to relate oneself to others. The infant is born with drives whose urgency is directed toward relating himself to others and to have others relate themselves to him. Life is social and man is born to be social, that is, cooperative, an interdependent part of a whole, a working, interacting part of a community. Again I should like to quote Alfred Adler's mature judgment here:

The individual's proper development can only progress if he lives and strives as a part of the whole. The shallow objections of individualistic systems have no meaning as against this view. I could go still further and show how all our functions are calculated to bind the single individual to the community, and not to destroy the fellowship of man with man. The act of seeing means to receive and make fruitful all that falls on the retina. This is not simply a physiological process; it shows that man is a part of a whole that gives and takes. In seeing, hearing, and speaking, we bind ourselves to one another. Man only sees, hears, and speaks rightly when he is linked to others by his interest in the external world. His reason, his common sense, forms the basis of his control of cooperation, of absolute truth, and aims at eternal rightness. Our aesthetic sense and views—perhaps the strongest powers that impel to great achievements—have an eternal value only when they lead to the well-being of humanity in the direction of the evolutionary stream. All our bodily and mental functions are rightly, normally, and healthily developed insofar as they are imbued with sufficient social feeling and are fitted for cooperation.

When we speak of virtue, we mean that a person plays his part; when we speak of vice, we mean that he interferes with cooperation. I can, moreover, point out that all that constitutes a failure is so because it obstructs social feeling, whether children, neurotics, criminals, or suicides are in question. In every case it can be seen that a contribution is lacking. No isolated persons are to be found in the whole history of humanity. The evolution of humanity was only possible because mankind was a community.

And again:

If the person understood how in evading the demands of evolution, he had gone astray, then he would give up his present course and join the general mass of humanity.

All the problems of human life demand capacity for cooperation and preparation for it—the visible signs of social feeling. In this disposition courage and happiness are included, and they are to be found nowhere else.[66]

[66] A. Adler, *Social Interest: A Challenge to Mankind*, Putnam, New York, 1938, pp. 282–283 and 284.

"I" VERSUS "YOU"

As GALT HAS POINTED OUT, THE FUNDA-
mental unit of social motivation and behavior is not the
person but the group.[67] This, however, does not mean
that the person no more represents the unit of social
behavior than the discrete reflex represents the unit of
physiological behavior. Because of his capacity for novel
and spontaneous behavior he represents a great deal
more.

The infant is not born with an ego. It acquires its self
from other selves long before it is aware of its own self.
Is not this an interesting fact? Its ego, its self, develops
only as the infant comes to recognize and adjust to reality. It is clearly not egocentric to begin with. What is

[67] W. Galt, "The Principle of Cooperation in Behavior," *Quarterly Review of Biology*, vol. 15, 1940, pp. 401–410.

usually confused with egocentricity are the generalized dependency needs of the infant which require satisfaction. But such satisfaction is not the demand of an organized ego, for the infant has no ego. The evidence, on the other hand, suggests that it is conditioned to become egocentric by processes of culturalization which emphasize egocentricity. In the cultures of the Western world particularly, the process of socialization, while binding the person to his group, has actually the effect of rendering the person functionally asocial. The child is trained in what is expected of him and what he may expect of others. But this training, as Galt points out,

is subsequent and parallel to a process in which there is a weaning of the child from the sense of biological continuity and solidarity with his kind, and the establishment within him of a sense of personal identity, motivation and authority which of its nature must be in conflict with the identity and motivation of others of his social group. Expressed differently, the total social behavioral pattern which is the biological heritage of the human infant, as it is of other animal species, is disrupted, and an undue individuation takes place. This individuation, which in the course of time sets up an autonomous individual with private hopes, desires, wishes, gains and losses, of necessity brings about severe conflict when the desires of two or more elements or individuals happen to interfere with one another. The incentives to behavior have inadvertently become tied up with the individual as an arbitrary centre of action and motivation rather than with the social group as such a centre.[68]

The workers at the Lifwynn Foundation, under the leadership of the late Trigant Burrow, found after many years of investigating and analyzing the so-called normal behavior of men in so-called normal communities, that "the normal individual, like the neurotic, was . . . constantly thinking and acting in terms of his individualized self. He has established an image of himself as

_____
[68] *Ibid.*, p. 405.

an isolated unit of behavior with private values, wishes and motivations, and this image dominates his social interrelations." [69] As Burrow says:

> In a word, the individual neurosis is but an exaggeration of "normality." It is but an expression, in miniature, of the social neurosis. Man is suffering from an organismic dislocation from the environment, from an "I"-complex or "I"-persona. The partitive sovereignty of the separate self. The result is a divisiveness of function, in which dissociation and conflict assume supremacy over the organism's unity and centralization of function. Man's relation to man becomes disordered through the subordination of the human organism to the conditioned artificial affects and prejudices of the "I"-persona. This social mood is divisive to its core, inciting each person to compete with others in the interest of the self. The principle upon which this divisive socially conditioned mood operates is I-versus-you.[70]

In such persons the central principle of creative motivation, the drive to realize the social feeling that is within them, becomes, if not blocked, then seriously disordered. The personality develops divisively and may become seriously fragmented. At any rate, it largely loses its power to co-ordinate, to unify, and to operate as a whole. In Adler's words: "It is always the want of social feeling, whatever be the name one gives it—living in fellowship, cooperation, humanity, or even the ideal-ego—which causes an insufficient preparation for all the problems of life. In the presence of a problem, this imperfect preparation gives rise to the thousand-fold forms that express physical and mental inferiority and insecurity." [71]

The suppressed voices of our inner consciousness tell

---

[69] *Ibid.*, p. 407.

[70] Burrow, "The Social Neurosis: A Study in 'Clinical Anthropology,'" *Philosophy of Science*, vol. 16, 1949, pp. 25–40.

[71] A. Adler, *Social Interest: A Challenge to Mankind,* Putnam, New York, 1938, p. 110.

us what we ought to be, of the life we have not lived, but could have lived had not something, we know not quite what, happened to determine otherwise. That "something" is the conditioning process to which we were exposed as infants and children. It is that which has made us, in the Western world, the partitive, disordered, hostile, egocentric creatures we have become. We are out of line with our evolutionary destiny, which is integration and cooperation, *not* disintegration and disoperation. On the personal, the community, national, and international planes, the effects are the same of an "I"-persona conditioning, namely, disorder, disease, and disoperation. To quote Burrow once more:

It is useless to essay a policy of social and economic cooperation on a non-cooperative basis of motivation. We will achieve a pattern of social cooperation and harmony among individuals and nations only when we have accepted the pattern on internal balance and coordination within the organism of man as a species. As things stand today, in this world of division and conflict, the war we have fought will have been fought in vain. It will have been no less vain than the many political and economic wars that have preceded it. Vain too must be the unilateral program of peace that will issue out of it. All our international covenants, all our external diplomatic treaties, all the peace programs yet to be devised must remain forever unavailing if our behavior dichotomies and antagonisms are ultimately traceable to a functional brain-twist that is internal to the organism of man as a race.[72]

The functional brain-twist is the "I"-persona conditioning of the frontal lobes which opposes itself to man's innate drives toward its polar counterpart, cooperation.

This writer agrees with Adler that

A careful consideration of individual and collective existence, both past and present, shows us the struggle of mankind for a

---

[72] Burrow, *op. cit.*

stronger social feeling. One can scarcely fail to see that humanity is conscious of this problem and is impressed by it. Our present-day burdens are the result of the lack of a thorough social education. It is the pent-up social feeling in us that urges us to reach a higher stage and to rid ourselves of the errors that mark our public life and our own personality. This social feeling exists within us and endeavors to carry out its purpose; it does not seem strong enough to hold its own against all opposing forces. The justified expectation persists that in a far-off age, if mankind is given enough time, the power of social feeling will triumph over all that opposes it. Then it will be as natural to man as breathing. For the present the only alternative is to understand and to teach that this will inevitably happen.[73]

One point upon which one might disagree with Adler is the last. It is perhaps dangerous to suggest that social feeling will inevitably triumph. On the other hand, if we go on as we have been doing, the chances are fairly high that we will exterminate ourselves. What is necessary is to understand and to teach the implications of the facts as we have come to know them, and what it is that needs to be done by way of emotional re-education.

Furthermore, a point which Adler overlooked, is that the harmonic, cooperative life in which social feeling does appear to be almost as natural as breathing has been achieved by several human groups—groups whom we used to call "savage," then "primitive," and now, thanks to the intervention of the anthropologist, "non-literate peoples." The best known examples of such groups are to be found among the Australian aborigines and the Eskimos.

The Australian aborigines knew neither the domestication of animals nor agriculture. They were food-gatherers and hunters and were generally regarded as among the technologically most primitive of living peoples. Yet

---

[73] A. Adler, *Social Interest: A Challenge to Mankind*, Putnam, New York, 1938, p. 285.

this nonliterate people (actually there were many different tribes, but the following statements hold true for all of them) lived in peace and harmony with their fellows, were quite unacquainted with war, and never did anything for the profit-motive. On the contrary, the socialization process took such a form that the child grew up to be a happy, joyous, secure person, who rarely, if ever, did anything without thinking of the consequences of his acts for his fellows.[74]

Similarly, all who have known the Eskimos of the Arctic and Alaska have been impressed by their complete cooperation and sense of personal responsibility to their fellows. Numerous books, from Stefansson through Peter Freuchen to Gontran de Poncins, have been written about the Eskimos and their way of life. Many a sophisticated, and many a simple, white man has fallen under their spell and settled among them.[75] Missionaries who have gone out to save the souls of the aborigines of Australia and the aborigines of the Far North have been known to say that it was not the souls of the aborigines which needed saving but those of the white men among them.

There are many other nonliterate, and some literate, peoples who exhibit a highly developed and sensitive awareness of their cooperative relation to their fellow men.[76]

---

[74] R. M. and C. H. Berndt, *The World of the First Australians*, University of Chicago Press, 1965; A. P. Elkin, *The Australian Aborigines*, Doubleday, New York, 1964.

[75] V. Stefansson, *My Life With the Eskimo*, Macmillan, New York, 1913.

[76] See E. M. Thomas, *The Harmless People*, Knopf, New York, 1959; K. Read, *The High Valley*, Scribners, 1965; D. Maybury-Lewis, *The Savage and the Innocent*, World, Cleveland, 1965; M. Bates and D. Abbott, *Coral Island*, Scribners, New York, 1958.

Foreigners who have dwelt among these peoples have frequently commented on the delightful breeding of the children and their sunny personalities. Anthropologists have long known that this is indeed a fact, and that it is largely the result of the permissiveness and low frequency of frustration to which these children are exposed. Such children tend to grow into secure, well-integrated adult personalities. The institutions of these societies, the social arrangements, that is to say, for maintaining the structure of the society, serve to maintain the security of the personality by the assurance which they afford it in terms of nonfrustrative, cooperative support.

In a book as short as this it is not possible to treat of these cultures at any length. The interested reader may, however, read further on this subject in the works listed below.[77]

The view that the child is born egocentric, evil, in "sin," is widely held, and it is nothing more than a projection upon the child of our own conditioning in egocentricity, in evil, in "sin." The alleged innate depravity of the child is not supported by the facts. The facts, on the contrary, show that the child is born as an actively cooperating organism. Charlotte Bühler has pointed out that cooperative behavior among children is more basic than competitive response, finding that the latter type

[77] S. S. Sargent and M. W. Smith (editors), *Culture and Personality,* The Viking Fund, New York, 1949; Ashley Montagu, *Coming into Being Among the Australian Aborigines,* Dutton, New York, 1937; W. Dennis, *The Hopi Child,* Appleton-Century, New York, 1940; D. Leighton and C. Kluckhohn, *Children of the People: The Navaho and His Individual Development,* Harvard University Press, Cambridge, 1947; A. Kardiner, *The Individual and His Society,* Columbia University Press, New York, 1939.

of response in her group of observed children did not make its appearance till about the third year.[78]

All observers have found that hostile responses in the child tend to increase as it grows older.[79]

From her vast experience, Bender finds that, far from being inborn, hostility in the child "is a symptom complex resulting from deprivations which are caused by developmental discrepancies in the total personality structure such that the constructive patterned drives for action in the child find inadequate means of satisfaction and result in amplification or disorganization of the drives into hostile or destructive aggression." "The child," she writes, "acts as though there were an inherent awareness of his needs and there is thus the expectation of having them met. A failure in this regard is a deprivation and leads to frustration and a reactive aggressive response." [80]

Indeed, the creativeness of the organism is directed toward maturation in terms of cooperation. Bender calls it "the inherent capacity or drive for normality." And she says, "The emphasis on the inborn or instinctive features of hostility, aggression, death wishes, and the negative emotional experiences represents a onesided approach which has led our students of child psychology astray."

---

[78] C. Bühler, "*Die ersten sozialen Verhaltungsweisen des Kindes,*" *Soziologische und Psychologische Studien über das erste Lebensjahr*, Fischer, Jena, 1927; C. Bühler, "Spontaneous Reactions of Children in the First Two Years," *Proceedings and Papers of the 9th International Congress of Psychology*, 1929, pp. 99–100.

[79] M. J. Muste and D. F. Sharpe, "Some Influential Factors in the Determination of Aggressive Behavior in Pre-school Children," *Child Development*, vol. 18, 1947, pp. 11–28.

[80] L. Bender, "Genesis of Hostility in Children," *American Journal of Psychiatry*, vol. 105, 1948, pp. 241–245.

Abraham Maslow writes, "I find children, up to the time they are spoiled and flattened out by the culture, nicer, better, more attractive human beings than their elders, even though they are of course more 'primitive' than their elders. The 'taming and transforming' that they undergo seem to hurt rather than help. It was not for nothing that a famous psychologist once defined adults as 'deteriorated children.'" "Could it be possible," Maslow inquires, "that what we need is a little *more* primitiveness and a little less taming?" [81]

The infant soon learns that in order to be satisfied, in order to be loved, he too must satisfy, he too must love, he must satisfy the requirements of others, he must cooperate, he must actually give up or postpone the satisfaction of certain desires if he is to achieve satisfaction in others and if he is to retain the love of those whose love he needs. This, too, is a recognizable adult pattern of behavior which takes its origin in early experiences. From the beginning, this pattern of behavior provides the most fundamentally important means by which the socialization of the organism is achieved. First, through love as a feeling of belongingness (security), and second, through love as authority, the authority of the affectionate tie. "I belong to this family, and it is because these people love me that I belong. I like to belong, therefore I must obey them and retain their love so that I may continue to belong." This is what the child resolves for himself though he may never give conscious expression to the thought. The relationships within his family condition the personal relationships throughout his life. "They are loaded with affection and carry the

[81] A. Maslow, "Our Maligned Animal Nature," *Journal of Psychology*, vol. 28, 1949, pp. 273–278. See also K. M. Banham, "The Development of Affectionate Behavior in Infancy," *Journal of Genetic Psychology*, vol. 76, 1950, pp. 283–289.

burden of giving to each a *place*—a sense of belonging, a meaning to the process of arriving and being." [82]

Outside the family, as a "grown-up," he secures the approval (love) of his fellows by conforming to the standards of the group. This is the family pattern repeated on a less intensive more extensive scale. To conform means the willingness to forego certain satisfactions in order to obtain others, to suffer a certain amount of deprivation and thwarting of satisfactions as a discipline which may ultimately lead to what are socially esteemed as greater rewards. A certain degree of conflict, repression, and aggressiveness are the consequences of such experiences both in the family and in the group in all cultures.

A conformity that is based on love will be free to develop into nonconformities, for the mentally healthy individual will not be bound to standards that conflict with his view of what is right. It is the unloved individual who fears to depart from group standards, who anxiously cleaves to those of his group. Those who have been adequately loved feel free to look out upon and embrace the world with interest and compassion. [83] They brook no hostilities to human diversity, and are opposed to any form of downgrading standardization. They see likeness and unity in difference, and do not equate unity with uniformity. They regard differences as points of interest, as complementary and not as antagonistic, as the means, indeed, of a more abundant common life, of sharing and fellowship.

---

[82] James Plant, *Personality and the Cultural Pattern*, The Commonwealth Fund, 1937, p. 267.

[83] T. W. Adorno, E. Frenkel-Brunswik, D. J. Levenson, and R. Nevitt Sanford, *The Authoritarian Personality*, Harper, New York, 1950; James G. Martin, *The Tolerant Personality*, Wayne University Press, Detroit, 1964.

Conformity to group standards concerned with the development of human values and the fulfillment of the individual demands a creative participation, a testing, and a self-giving, which is the very opposite of that bigoted unquestioning conformity in which so many have been frighteningly conditioned.[84]

[84] H. H. Remmers and D. H. Radler, *The American Teenager*, Bobbs-Merrill Co., Indianapolis, 1957; Philip E. Jacob, *Changing Values in College*, Harper, New York, 1957; Winston White, *Beyond Conformity*, Free Press, New York, 1961.

THE NEED TO LOVE

THE INFANT NOT ONLY NEEDS TO BE LOVED, but quite as much as he needs to be loved he needs to love others. It is due to the poverty of our language, which faithfully reflects the inadequacies of our understanding of these matters, that we are forced to distinguish between the need to be loved and the need to love others. That need is unitary, and is only arbitrarily divisible. The division may be convenient, but it should never be forgotten that it is arbitrary. It is not possible to want to be loved without wanting to love others.

When, then, it is said that the infant needs to be loved it should concomitantly be understood that the infant also wants to love others. It is important to understand that the infant's need for love is not adequately satisfied unless it receives the necessary stimulations for the development of its capacity to love. It may, indeed, be said that the child's need for love from others is important principally because that love is the most significant developer of its own capacity to love others. The child learns to love others by being loved.

There has been a tendency to regard the newborn infant as a passive utterly dependent creature who is entirely devoted to receiving without in any way giving. This view is wholly false, for from the very outset the child grows by striving to give, and it is biologically equipped to do so from the moment of birth.

The nursing couple, mother and infant, confer basic benefits upon one another—for when a baby is born a mother is or should also be born. In the reciprocal relationship in which mother and child are involved it becomes increasingly evident that the gift they make to each other is their own selves—selves that are striving for fulfillment and development. The gift unaccompanied by the committal of the giver is arid, a mere thing unenriched by the human meaning to the recipient of the giver. The infant expects others to become involved with him, and he is profoundly involved in others. The less others are with him the more he strives to be with them. We have already seen that those infants who are so isolated that they have no one with whom to be involved tend to become apathetic and waste away. The human situation is involvement in others in increasingly healthier relationships. And by health I mean the ability to love, the ability to work, and the ability to serve.

The self grows by the increasing interactive involvement with others. Whether the self develops as an affectionate one or as more or less defective in that quality, will depend largely, if not entirely, upon whether its experience of such qualities from others, especially the mother, has been of a loving kind.

Every neurosis has at its core the failure of healthy

involvement, of relatedness to others. The foundations for this failure, as Freud pointed out, are laid within the first six years or so of life. This is but another way of saying that there has been a failure of the developing ego to receive adequate satisfactions.

The ego develops in health only when it receives an adequate regimen of satisfactions. The greatest of these is the opportunity afforded the developing human being to exercise his capacity for love. Never has this been better said than by George Chapman (1559–1634), the Tudor poet and playwright, who in his play *All Fools,* probably produced in 1599, writes:

> I tell thee, Love is Nature's second sun
> Causing a spring of virtues where he shines;
> And as without the Sun, the World's great eye,
> All colours, beauties, both of art and Nature,
> Are given in vain to men; so without love
> All beauties bred in women are in vain,
> All virtues born in men lie buried;
> For love informs them as the Sun doth colours;
> And as the Sun, reflecting his warm beams
> Against the earth, begets all fruits and flowers;
> So love, fair shining in the inward man,
> Brings forth in him the honourable fruits
> Of valour, wit, virtue, and haughty thoughts,
> Brave resolution, and divine discourse.

FISSION VERSUS FUSION

As we have pointed out, the failure to develop social competence is due to the privation of love suffered by the infant during the first six years or so of life. We are thus led to conclude that in order to be successfully social, one must have learned to love by having been loved; that, indeed, society is based on love, in fact *is* but a developed form of love. That where hatreds exist in any persons within any society we may be sure that they, too, are due to love, for hatred is love frustrated. Aggression is but a technique or mode of seeking love.

Love is in its essence, in its beginning and end, social. It arises out of the satisfaction of the self-preservative or basic needs of the organism in the primary dependent relationship to the parent, and it demands always the presence of other persons or their substitutes in order to function adequately.

Man's need for society and his need for love are one and the same thing. Ian Suttie, in a brilliant book, has suggested that "play, cooperation, competition and culture-interests generally are substitutes for the mutually caressing relationship of child and mother. *By these substitutes we put the whole social environment in the place once occupied by the mother.*" [85]

The organism is born with an innate need for love, with a need to respond to love, to be good, cooperative. This is, I believe, now established beyond any shadow of doubt. Whatever is opposed to love, to goodness, and to cooperation is disharmonic, unviable, unstable, and malfunctional—evil. Were the infant's needs adequately satisfied, he could not help being good—that is, loving. All of man's natural inclinations are toward the development of goodness, toward the continuance of states of goodness and the discontinuance of unpleasant states. As Ralph Lillie has pointed out:

A property of the good (in the universal or Platonic sense) is that unconscious effort is inevitably directed toward its continuance (since it is the object of desire) while evil, the immediately or ultimately painful, is a feature of reality which conscious effort tends to remove or overcome. The former has thus within itself a property or character which favors its continuance; the latter is inherently unstable. Analysis shows that stability in all highly diversified or composite systems requires harmonious relations (relations of balance or equilibrium) between the different components and activities . . . modern biology recognizes that integration between different types of individuals as seen in the cooperative relations between units in human and animal communities (or even between different species of animals or plants), is as much of a factor in survival and evolution as is conflict. The avoidance of useful conflict, and the subordination of individual interests to the interest of the integrated whole which includes the individuals, would thus seem to be rational aims for conscious beings; and these aims have the further sanc-

---

[85] Ian D. Suttie, *The Origins of Love and Hate*, Kegan Paul, London, 1935, p. 16.

tion of religion when the whole is conceived in its character as ultimate value or deity.[86]

The biological basis of love consists in the organism's drive to satisfy its basic needs in a manner which causes it to feel secure. Love *is* security. Mere satisfaction of basic needs is not enough. Needs must be satisfied in a particular manner, in a manner which is emotionally as well as physically satisfying.

To repeat, the biological basis of love lies in the organism's ever-present urge to feel secure, and it would appear that the basis of all social life has its roots in this integral of all the basic needs which is expressed as the need for security, and that the only way in which this need can be satisfied is by love.

It is a discovery of the greatest possible significance for mankind that the ethical conception of love independently arrived at by almost all existing peoples is no mere creation of man but is grounded in the biological structure of man as a functioning organism. The implications of this discovery are of the very greatest importance, for it means that man's organic potentialities are so organized as to demand but one kind of satisfaction alone, a satisfaction which ministers to man's need for love, which registers love, which is given in terms of love—a satisfaction which is defined by the one word, *security.* That is what the human being seeks all his life, and society, culture, and man's institutions, however inefficient some of them may be, all exist to secure that one fundamental satisfaction. The emotional need for love is as definite and compelling as the need for food.

---

[86] Ralph S. Lillie, "The Psychic Factor in Living Organisms," *Philosophy of Science*, vol. 10, 1943, pp. 262–270. See also the same author's *General Biology and Philosophy of Organism*, University of Chicago Press, Chicago, 1945; Edmund W. Sinnott, *The Biology of the Spirit,* Viking, New York, 1955.

The basic needs of man must be satisfied in order that he may function on the organic level. But in order that he may function satisfactorily on the social plane, the most fundamental of the basic social needs must be satisfied in an emotionally adequate manner for personal security or equilibrium.

It has been shown that when the needs of the developing social organism are inadequately satisfied, that is, where there have been too many frustrations—thwartings of expected satisfactions—where there has been a privation of love, the organism becomes disordered, anxious, tense, fearful, and hostile. This, in fact, is more or less the state into which most human beings in the Western world today have fallen.

Security, it should be clear, is but another word for love. It should never be confused with that material satiation and ease of circumstance or smug intellectual self-satisfaction, which so many pursue under the mistaken impression that in this way security will be achieved. "Life, liberty, and the pursuit of happiness" cannot be achieved by any other means than love. The search for security of the unloving kind is devastatingly harmful to the achievement of healthy human values. No amount of perfection of means can ever offset the damage done by confused goals. What is essentially meaningful about man is that he is a spiritual creature, and that as such it is principally spiritual victories that can be of importance to him. Material victories have their time and place, but they must always remain secondary to man's spiritual conquests, conquests principally of himself. Else the victor is in danger of ending up by belonging to the spoils. By "spiritual" I do not mean "religious" in any formal sense, but simply progress in goodness. And by "goodness" I mean essentially the ability to love, and the ability to experience and to respond with deepening sensitivity to the world in which one lives. Not as an echo, but with a voice of one's own.

In the preceding pages it has been suggested that the biological basis of cooperation has its origins in the same sources as social behavior, namely, in the process of reproduction. It has been shown that social, cooperative behavior is simply the continuation and development of the parent-offspring relationship. Cooperative, social behavior is therefore as old as life itself, and the direction of evolution has, in man, been increasingly directed toward the fuller development of cooperative behavior.

Cooperative behavior clearly has great survival value. When social behavior is not cooperative, it is diseased. The dominant principle which informs all behavior that is biologically healthy is love. Without love there can be no healthy social behavior, cooperation, or security. To love thy neighbor as thyself is not simply good text material for Sunday morning sermons but perfectly sound biology.

Men who do not love one another are sick—sick not from any disease arising within themselves but from a disease which has been enculturated within them by the false values of their societies. Belief in false values which condition the development of the person, in competition instead of cooperation, in narrow selfish interests instead of altruism, in atomism (especially hydrogen-bombism) instead of universalism, in the value of money instead of the value of man, such beliefs represent man turning upon all that is innately oriented toward goodness in him.

Thus, in our society, there are conflicting and mutually irreconcilable institutions which put too great a strain upon the adaptive capacities of most persons. The

Christian ethic of love in relation to the business ethic of competition or "free enterprise," for example. On the one hand, we expose our children to a system of ideal teachings which we call Christianity, and with which we more or less endeavor to inoculate them, while, on the other hand, we increasingly expose them to precepts and examples which place a high value upon competition. We pay lip service to spiritual values but place our faith in material possessions. Our prices and our values have become sadly confused. Is laisser-faire capitalism, free enterprise, compatible with Christianity, with co-operation, with love? The individual may never explicitly ask himself such questions, but there is not the least doubt that they create dilemmas within him which he is never able to solve, and which substantially contribute to rendering him the problem, the unsolved problem he becomes.

Man's drives toward mutuality and cooperativeness may be suppressed, but so long as man continues to exist, they cannot be destroyed, for these are traits which are part of his protoplasm. His combativeness and competitiveness arise primarily from the frustration of his need to cooperate. These are important facts to bear in mind at a time when all the surface evidence seems to point in a contrary direction. The word of the moment may be "fission"—whether with respect to physics or human affairs—but "fusion" comes much closer to reflecting man's natural behavior patterns.

Science points the way to survival and happiness for all mankind through love and cooperation. Do what we will, our drives toward goodness are as biologically determined as are our drives towards breathing. Our highly endowed potentialities for social life have been used to pervert and deny their very nature, and this has led us close to the brink of disaster, a disaster which spells doom unless we realize what we have done and take the proper steps to undo it before it is too late. For we cannot, without destroying ourselves, deny the power of these developmental drives which we share with all life and which have reached their highest development in our potentialities as human beings.

Our world at the present time is at the mercy of criminally irresponsible adventurers, political opportunists, and cynical and complacent men who have grown old in the ways of self-interest and ultranationalism. Unless their place is taken by men of understanding and humility, whose guiding principle is love, the world of man is doomed.

The life of every human being is a part of our own, for we are involved in mankind. Each one of us is responsible for the other. It was Dostoevski who said, "Each of us is responsible for everything to everyone else." That is what we now know. It is up to us to do something with that knowledge.

Part III

The Improvement of
Human Relations

THE FOURTH *R*

Wнат can be done should be suffi-
ciently clear from the preceding pages. What man needs
is a change in attitudes of mind. He must reorient his
development and conduct in the direction of cooperation, of love, for it is development in those terms that
contributes most to the realization of man's health and
welfare. All human beings want to be good. All human
beings want to be happy. Their biological drives are
oriented in the direction of those ends. But most human
beings in our culture are confused about means and
ends in doing good and in securing happiness. Evil
means are often used to secure "good" ends, and so-
called "good" means are sometimes used to secure evil
ends. If man can but be persuaded to try living in cooperation with his fellow men, he will discover that it
is no more difficult to do so than to say so. For the drives

toward cooperation are all there within him, and they are his *dominant* drives. Man has but to give them the opportunity to express themselves.

The wonderful thing about the principle of cooperation is that in addition to proving the value of cooperation as a way of life, it also proves that cooperation, love, is *a means which when applied to human relations is the most conducive of all to the establishment of good human relations.*

Goodness is behavior calculated to confer survival benefits in a creatively enlarging manner upon others.

It is the belief of this writer that, in addition to what each person can himself do, here and now, the best results may be secured through the long-term agency of education. For this reason the final part of this book will be devoted to a consideration of the improvement of human relations through education.

In our schools we teach the three *r*'s; the fourth *r*, relations, *human relations,* it has been said, we do not teach. I think this is no more true than to say that what is wrong with most people of the Western world today is that they have no values. Unfortunately, the trouble with most of us is not that we have no values but that we have too many of the wrong kind. Similarly, it is not true to say that we fail to teach human relations in our schools. We do teach such relations not only in a negative way but we teach them in an unmistakably positive way. And it is, on the whole, a way which is of the most unfortunate kind.

Organized instruction in human relations, when it is not left to the coach on the football or baseball team, is generally more honored in the breach than in the observance. But unorganized instruction in human relations occurs in all schools. From the principal to the janitor, children learn how to behave in relation to others—not so much from what is said as from what these preceptors consciously and unconsciously do. Example is stronger than precept, and imitation is the most immediate form of learning. Words have no meaning other than the action they produce. And in our schools words are activated by what the teachers believe. From every standpoint, then, it is important that teachers, the unacknowledged legislators of the world, shall believe in the right things. For unless they do so, their words and conduct, no matter how noble the sentiments they are supposed to express, will be recognized for the counterfeit coin they are.

There are today, for example, many teachers in our schools who are teaching race prejudice to their pupils. They do this not by means of prepared courses in the subject but by their attitudes—by a look, an expression, an inflection of the voice, or the weighting of a word. Though they have never been formulated in so many words, the views of such teachers on the subject of race and race relations are clearly understood by, and exert a considerable influence upon, their pupils. Such teachers do not belong in a school. The principal function of the teacher is, or should be, to help prepare the child for living a humane and cooperative life, not to infect his mind with the antihuman virus of racism.[87]

No one should ever be permitted to become a teacher of the young unless by temperament, attitudes, and training he is fitted to do so. The teacher is the most important of all the public servants of the community: for what service can be more important to the community than the kind of molding of the mind and channeling of the social behavior of the future citizen which the

---

[87] See Samuel Lowy, *Co-Operation, Tolerance, and Prejudice*, Routledge, London, 1948; Gordon Allport, *The Nature of Prejudice*, Addison-Wesley, Cambridge, 1953.

teacher is able to direct? The anything but princely stipends with which he is rewarded for his services suggest that our society does not recognize the true value or function of the teacher.[88]

The school, as it is at present constituted, is a place of instruction. It is not really a place of education in the proper sense of that word—in the sense of nourishing and causing to grow the unique potentialities of the individual—which is the original meaning of *educare*. In conformity with the requirements of a burgeoning industrial civilization, techniques and technology are at a premium. What can be used to succeed in such a society becomes that which is most emphasized during the learning period, the rest is sheer luxury. From such a standpoint it is but natural that we should come to believe that the function of the school is essentially to teach the three *r*'s in terms of the crude needs of an industrial civilization.

Clearly, values here are sadly mixed. They are the values of the world's largest industrial civilization. The value "success" in such a civilization is measured in terms of dollars. A man's worth in such a civilization tends to become not his quality but his quantity, quantity of dollars, possessions.

Validation of success in terms of externals has become the mark of our civilization. In such a value system, human relations take on the ethical values of the salesman. The idols of the market place reign supreme. Competition is the most powerful law. The competitive personality governed by the ideals of an industrial society must always be out in front. He must be better than others, for to be so yields the greatest returns. In the world of

---

[88] D. Louise Sharp (editor), *Why Teach?*, Holt, New York, 1957.

a person so conditioned, it is taken for granted that some persons are inferior to others in their capacity to achieve. To most such persons the notion that there are whole groups of mankind that are unimprovably inferior is not only acceptable but indispensably necessary, for it constitutes at once a proof of the validity of the system and an incentive to go ahead and reap its benefits. It is a fully fledged belief in the doctrine of the survival of the fittest. The fit are those who are going to succeed or who have already succeeded, while the unfit are those who are not going to succeed, and it is, of course, most convenient and useful to know beforehand what groups of men are *not* going to succeed.

The very large amount of mental disorder, nervous tension, conflict, fear, anxiety, frustration, and insecurity which occurs in Western society is largely due to the failure of the values in which we have been conditioned since infancy—false values by which we seek to live. The fact is that human beings cannot be false to each other and to themselves without breaking down under the strain, however often they may attempt to relieve themselves of their frustrations and anxieties by attacking their scapegoats.

Man is born for cooperation, not for competition or conflict. This is a basic discovery of modern science. It confirms a discovery made some two thousand years ago by one Jesus of Nazareth, and by others before him. In a word: it is the principle of love which embraces all mankind. It is the principle of humanity, of one world, one brotherhood of peoples.

The measure of a person's humanity is the extent and intensity of his love for mankind. That measure is not the extent or intensity of his knowledge of the three r's. If mankind is to be saved, it can be done only by replacing the values of industrial technology with those of humanity, of cooperation, of love. It is only when humanity is in control that technology in the service of humanity will occupy its proper place in the scheme of things. A most important and immediate task is to make the people understand this. It is the duty of everyone capable of doing so to undertake this task. There must be a complete revaluation and reorientation of our values.

The school beyond all else must be considered as a place of education in the art and science of being a person, the practice of human relations. Let us recall here the words of Franklin Delano Roosevelt from the 1945 Jefferson Day speech which, so tragically, he did not live to deliver:

the mere conquest of our enemies is not enough. We must go on to do all in our power to conquer the doubts and the fears, the ignorance and the greed which made this horror possible.

Today, we are faced with the pre-eminent fact that *if civilization is to survive, we must cultivate the science of human relationships—the ability of all peoples, of all kinds, to live together and work together in the same world at peace.*

Without in any way slighting the important influence which the home constitutes, I believe that the school must be considered as a most important agency in the teaching of the art and science of human relations. We must shift the emphasis from the three r's to the fourth r, human relations, and place it first, foremost, and always in that order of importance, as the principal reason for the existence of the school. It must be clearly understood, once and for all time, that human relations are the most important of all relations. Upon this understanding must be based all our educational policies. We must train for humanity, and training in reading, writing, and arithmetic must be given in a manner calculated to serve the ends of that humanity. For all the knowledge in the world is worse than useless if it is not humanely understood and humanely used. An intelligence that is not humane is the most dangerous thing in the world.

Our teachers must, therefore, be specially qualified to teach human relations. The importance of their function must be recognized and suitably rewarded by a society anxious to encourage the entry of the best kind of people into the professional privilege of preparing human beings for the art of living. There can be no more important task than this. It is a task which demands qualities of the highest order. The teacher must be temperamentally fitted for his profession, and he should himself be an exemplar of the art of living and the practice of human relations. Children would learn more from such a teacher than from all the factually informed instructors in the world.

Are these specifications visionary? Certainly they will not be achieved if we think so. It is my belief not only that they can be achieved, but that it is our moral obligation to see that they are realized. Palliative piecemeal approaches are not enough. If we are to cure the disease, we must attend to its causes.

Prominent among these causes are the substitution of economics for humanity, the substitution of competition for cooperation, frustration of our children for the loving firmness which should be their right, of the piling up of unexpended aggressiveness within them, and the production of conflicts and insecurities incident to the structure of a competitive society—a society which, on the one hand, preaches brotherly love and, on the other, practices self-love and the denial of brotherhood.

Most human beings want to like, to love, their fellow men. Yet in their everyday lives they, for the most part, practice self-love and are more or less hostile toward all those whom they conceive to stand in their way. The reason for this tragic disparity between what they feel to be right and what they do is simply that the structure of this society is such that the life of the person becomes reduced to a competitive struggle for existence. Under such conditions, men everywhere tend to become nasty, brutish, and cruel. They become atomistic, selfish, individualistic. In such a situation it is hard for them to do otherwise, for the first law of life is and has always been self-preservation (the satisfaction of basic needs), and if the individual will not do everything in his power to gain security for himself, who will? Well might he echo that Talmudic voice which said: "If I am not for myself, who will be for me? If I am for myself only, what am I? If not now—when?"

But "If I am for myself only, what am I?"

In such a society man lives for himself alone; he is forced to. The right of other persons to existence is acknowledged in so far as it contributes to his security. Those persons or groups who may be conceived as constituting an obstacle to that achievement therefore evoke hostile and aggressive responses. Yet these same persons know from such religious training as they may have received that such conduct is wrong and evil.

Were the conditions provided for such persons to lead the good life in harmony with all men, can there be the least doubt that they would take full advantage of those conditions?

In order to live the good life, it is first necessary to live. If the structure of society is such that it makes of life a struggle for bare physical existence, in which frustration and insecurity are maximized, in which the person is left to sink or swim entirely alone, the "good life" is equated with personal survival, and "a good time." In an industrial civilization with its emphasis on success in terms of material values, success is generally achieved in material terms at the expense of truly human values.

Western society, in short, does not encourage the development of goodness because goodness is not what that society is interested in. Goodness belongs to a frame of reference other than that in which we make our living. It belongs to the covert rather than to the overt part of our culture. What we need to do is to enthrone goodness, human relations, in the place at present occupied by economics. The idols of the market place must yield to those of humanity. The two are not incompatible, but it is foolish to put economics ahead of humanity, when economics belong in the service of humanity. A society such as ours, in which human relations are subordinated to the economic system, can rescue itself only by subordinating its economy to the purposes of human relations.

And this is the task that the schools must assist in undertaking, no less than the rescue of man from his debasing enslavement to the principles and practices of an acquisitive society.

One cannot love and respect anyone unless one has a genuine love and respect for oneself. This has nothing to do with egoism. It is the individualist who is the egoist. It is he who is lacking in genuine love and respect for himself, in contrast to the social person, who is interested in selfhood and not in selfishness. The guilt and frustration built up by the throttling of personal authenticity get in the way of the individualist's ability to love and respect others.

Self and society are reverse sides of the same coin. Self grows and becomes enriched and fulfilled only as it becomes sharable, social. Society flourishes as a function of selfhood or social persons. The individualist possesses only a spurious or crippled form of selfhood.

It is this that the Talmudic saying is trying to express: "If I am not for myself, who will be for me? If I am for myself only, what am I? If not now—when?" Self-responsibility is the basic law of human living. A man must first look to himself and to his own. But he also has to see his personal interests and responsibilities as opening into collective interests and responsibilities. The cosmos itself is the smallest frame of reference in which he may think, if he is to orient his life in the direction of human values. Self and society only exist together. "If not now —when?" The principle of self-responsibility, for self, society, and the world, has relevance only *now!* Fullness and bountiful living, the creation and development of self and society is possible only *now*. Never at some later date. One may not put off being human. In a very profound way all the wisdom and the whole secret of human relations is incorporated in this Talmudic saying.

Those who would have us believe that almost everything human beings are involved in is determined by economics are wrong. Certainly if you build a society on economic foundations and you make the whole superstructure dependent upon those foundations, economic determinism will be a most influentially operative principle. But only in a society which is so structured. The U.S.S.R. constitutes an example of such a society, and one which for that reason is humanly such a drab and abysmal failure. If you identify human nature with economics, with production, you make of a man a commodity, and you create a system of material values which readily lends itself to exploitation. When you build your society upon the foundation of human relations, as so many nonliterate societies have done, the processes of getting a living are cooperative; no one does anything for gain, the profit motive is nonexistent, and the individual feels secure in the knowledge that as long

114

as there is anything to eat, every member in the group will eat. The menace of insecurity is collectively eliminated and individual destitution unknown. The determinants of conduct in such a society stem from social organization and religion, from the human relations of the group, as do the determinants of economic behavior.[89]

The motives of human beings everywhere are human, *not* economic. They are made to become economic only in societies in which moneytheism or communism is the prevailing religion. If, then, we would establish a world of humanity, we must educate human motivations in terms of humanity and not of economics. We must remove economics as the dominant motive from human relations and make human relations the dominant motive in economics.

Let no one be deceived. Unless Western man is able to release himself from the degrading tyranny of his enslavement to the religion of economics, he is as certainly doomed to self-destruction as all the portents indicate. Man cannot live by bread alone. Physiologically, biologically, psychologically, and socially, he can retain his health and flourish only in love of, and cooperation with, his fellow man.[90]

A profit-motive, economic-struggle-for-existence society is a predatory society, a class-and-caste society, a divisive society, in which each person is forced into the role of an isolate preying upon and preyed upon by others. Economic security, power, and prestige are the

[89] Margaret Mead (editor), *Cooperation and Competition Among Primitive Peoples,* Beacon Press, Boston, 1961.

[90] Samuel Lowy, *Man and His Fellow Man,* Kegan Paul, London, 1944; E. Jordan, *The Good Life,* University of Chicago Press, 1949; M. A. R. Tuker, *Past and Future of Ethics,* Oxford University Press, 1938.

objectives which determine the motivations of men in such a society. Under such conditions men attempt to limit the opportunities for successful achievement to themselves. Few succeed and most are caused to fail. This is the chief result, as well as the cause, of class and caste distinctions. The frustration and aggressiveness so produced is enormous. Professor Robert K. Merton has brilliantly described the frustrative situation in our society.

It is only when a system of cultural values extols, virtually above all else, certain common symbols of success *for the population at large,* while its social structure rigorously restricts or completely eliminates access to approved modes of acquiring these symbols *for a considerable part of the same population,* that antisocial behavior ensues on a considerable scale. In other words, our egalitarian ideology denies by implication the existence of noncompeting groups and individuals in the pursuit of pecuniary success. The same body of success symbols is held to be desirable for all. These goals are held to *transcend class lines,* not to be bound by them, yet the actual social organization is such that there exist class differentials in the accessibility of these *common* success symbols. Frustration and thwarted aspiration lead to the search for avenues of escape from a culturally induced intolerable situation; or unrelieved ambition may eventuate in illicit attempts to acquire the dominant values. The American stress on pecuniary success and ambitiousness for all thus invites exaggerated anxieties, hostilities, neuroses, and antisocial behavior.[91]

Race prejudice and discrimination are among the consequences of such anarchic conditions, and these racial hostilities will not be removed until these conditions are removed. Hence, let it be clearly understood that teaching of the facts of race in the schools and elsewhere, intercultural programs, Springfield Plans, and the like, while they may help as palliatives, will not substantially

---

[91] R. K. Merton, "Social Structure and Anomie," *American Sociological Review,* vol. 3, 1938, p. 680.

solve the problem, though they may contribute toward its solution. The problem we have to solve is first and foremost the problem of how we can rebuild our society in terms of human values in which human relations are given a chance to function as they should. No matter what we teach in the schools concerning the equality of man, unless these teachings are provided with a social milieu in which they can be practiced, they will wilt and die in the breasts of those who are forced to adapt themselves to the world as they find it.

How, then, is the problem to be solved?

The answer is: Through social change. And who are to be the instruments of that social change? The answer to that is: The children who are to be the adult members of the next generation. How are they to be prepared for their task? First, by being adequately loved within the ambience of a firmness and a discipline that only love knows. They must be taught that freedom is responsibility, and that it will be their responsibility to do what they are able, everywhere, to improve the lot of man. Toward this end they will have to be taught how to utilize their minds, as the fine instruments they can become, for the creative interrogation and critical evaluation of the problems with which they will be confronted. To join learning to loving kindness, they will require to learn that sound thinking is as vitally important as sound loving, and that the two must always remain in feedback control of one another. That one can truly understand only those things that one loves, that holiness is where love dwells, and the promise of good, and that true civilization is the process, the art, of learning to be kind.

Human beings who are torn and distracted by internal insecurities and dissensions, doubts and anxieties, and conditioned to compete on weekdays and to love their neighbors on Sundays, cannot long endure. A people comprised of such persons must eventually founder on the rock of its own false values. External defenses can never make up for the lack of internal controls. What we need to do is to build internal controls in human beings so that they can withstand external pressures and maintain internal equilibrium. This cannot be done by doing violence to their nature. It can only be accomplished by strengthening those basic needs with which all human beings are born—not by frustrating them.

The evidence is overwhelming that when the child's basic needs are adequately satisfied, when, in other words, the child is loved, and it is exposed to the necessary but minimum amount of frustrations, no matter in what culture or class that child grows and develops, it tends to be a better equilibrated, less aggressive, more cooperative person than one who has not been adequately loved in childhood. We live by a pure flame within us. That flame is love. It is the source from which we draw and convey our warmth to others. It is the light which guides us in relation to our fellow men. It is the flame before which we warm the hands of life, and without which we remain cold all our lives. It is the light of the world. The light it casts enables us clearly to perceive our relation to our fellow men. It is for us to keep that flame burning, for if we fail to do that, there is a real danger that the light will go out of the world.

The critical social and educational problem of today is one of learning how shared relationships may be fostered and freedom of inquiry accelerated. It seems to me, first, that this must be done through the schools, and second that there must be a virtually complete change in our attitudes toward education. Scarcely anywhere in the world at the present time does there exist anything resembling education. What does exist is instruction—training in techniques and skills. What are we "educating" for? Obviously we are instructing our future citizens in what it takes to live in the world in which they find themselves. We are equipping them with technological skills, the skills it takes to maintain that world. More by default than by design, we teach them a kind of cracker-barrel human relations, to become echoes, as it were, of other stereotyped lives already lived. That is to say, in the most important of all relations, human relations, our educators fail most miserably. For what can be more important than human relations? What is all the instruction in the world worth if it is not accompanied and integrated by an understanding of man's responsibility to man? A holistic and humane, and a scientific, approach to education must begin with the basic assumption that values must in the long run be tested by their capacity to contribute to the happiness and creativeness of human beings living together. If we can find a basis in *fact* for what *should* be, we should at least be willing to give it a try.

I suggest, then, that our schools be transformed into institutes or schools for the study of the science and art of human relations. I mean that children be taught the theory and practice of human relations from their earliest years, and for this purpose, among other things, I would make the nursery school part of the public educational system. The three r's must be secondary to the primary purposes of human relations, for whatever is learned should be learned principally with reference to its significance for human relations, and always with the emphasis on cooperation, on shared relationships. Children should be taught not how to become the apes of their teachers and the uncritical bearers of their traditions, but how to evaluate humanely and critically the world in which they are living. They should be taught not only the overt but also the covert values of their society, not only what is right with their society and which they must maintain, but also what is wrong with it, and what it is going to be their job to put right, and how they may put what is wrong right.

I am often asked how such an undertaking could possibly be initiated. Don't I realize the enormous social inertia with which one would have to contend were one to attempt to develop such a program? Indeed, the inertia is considerable, and the difficulties are great, but they are by no means insuperable. It would be wonderful if one could commence with a community and work directly through the school system, and this should be the aim wherever and whenever possible, but failing that, a single teacher in a single classroom of a school, multiplied over many schools, could do valuable work in the desired direction. This would hardly make an impression were it to stop at a single classroom in a few schools, but the hope would be that, with constant awareness of the problem, the movement to teach human relations in the school would grow and spread.

As I have said, there is not too much time left. The tendency to equate economic liberty with democracy has helped to disguise the fact that many of our ideas and institutions are under constant threat from our very own selves, for persons who are in conflict with themselves, anxious and insecure, tend to be rigid in their ideas and in their behavior, as if to lean upon their rigidity as a rod in compensation for the reed of themselves. Such persons cannot be free, nor can they tolerate freedom in others. These are the kind of persons who tend to become totalitarians. We have been producing them in fairly large numbers in the United States and elsewhere. We need to stimulate educators in awakening to the full sense of their responsibility to make themselves acquainted with the latest findings of social biology, and to do something about applying those findings.

The possibilities for the development of cooperative human relations are enormous. They need only be recognized and dealt with intelligently. We must recognize that the competitive values of our culture put men in opposition to each other, and that under such conditions humanity does not prosper. The human infant is born with a highly developed system of needs which seek further development in terms of cooperation, *not* competition. Human nature is oriented in its primary thrust toward goodness. Human *nature* is good. It is human *nurture* that is bad. We need to conform human nurture to the requirements of human nature, and to disabuse mankind of the myth of the inherent naughtiness of humanity.[92]

It is personal influence that determines the size of life, not words. The abstract inconsideration of good intentions is not enough. Nor are the recurrent un-illuminating bows made toward distant horizons. Nor is the burning of incense at empty shrines. What needs to be done, needs to be done here and now. Every human being is a problem in search of a solution. We must ask ourselves the question whether we are going to continue to be part of the problem, or whether we are going to make ourselves a part of the solution.

---

[92] Ashley Montagu, *The Human Revolution,* World Publishing Co., Cleveland, 1965.

FURTHER READING

Aries, Philippe. *Centuries of Childhood.* Knopf, New York, 1962.
On man's changing attitudes toward the family and children.

Bay, Christian. *The Structure of Freedom.* Stanford University Press, Stanford, 1958.
A consideration of the freedom of man as an individual.

Benda, Clemens E. *The Image of Love.* Free Press, New York, 1961.
How the understanding of the meaning of love reveals man's nature.

Benedict, Ruth. *The Chrysanthemum and the Sword.* Houghton Mifflin, Boston, 1946.
A study of Japanese culture and personality.

Bishop, Claire H. *All Things Common.* Harper & Bros., New York, 1950.
The story of a remarkable experiment in community living.

Dixon, W. Macneile. *The Human Situation.* Longmans, New York, 1938.
One of the most beautiful books of its kind.

Dobzhansky, Th. *Mankind Evolving.* Yale University Press, New Haven, 1962.
On mankind in the continuing process of evolution.

Erikson, Erik H. *Childhood and Society.* 2nd ed. Norton, New York, 1963.
On the social significance of childhood.

Goudge, T. A. *The Ascent of Life.* Allen & Unwin, London, 1961.
A philosophical study of the theory of evolution.

Hollingshead, A. B. *Elmtown's Youth*. Wiley & Sons, New York, 1949.
The class system and its effect upon personality, as studied in a typical American town.

Korzybski, Alfred. *Manhood of Humanity*. 2nd ed. Institute of General Semantics, Lakeville, Conn., 1950.
On the theory and practice of directing human energies.

La Barre, Weston. *The Human Animal*. University of Chicago Press, 1954.
On the nature of man.

Matson, Floyd W. *The Broken Image*. Braziller, New York, 1964.
An exploration of the sciences of man in the modern world, with a reconstitution of the broken image.

Mead, Margaret. *And Keep Your Powder Dry*. 2nd ed. Morrow, New York, 1965.
On the development of American character.

Menaker, Esther & William. *Ego in Evolution*. Grove Press, New York, 1965.
On the evolution of the human psyche.

Miller, Hugh. *The Community of Man*. Macmillan, New York, 1949.

———. *Progress and Decline*. Ward Ritchie Press, Los Angeles, 1963.
On the creative evolution of man.

Montagu, Ashley. *The Human Revolution*. World Publishing Co., Cleveland, Ohio, 1965.

——— (editor). *Culture and the Evolution of Man*.
On the interaction between man's genetic constitution and culture in the evolution of humanity.

Patten, William. *The Grand Strategy of Evolution*. Badger, Boston, 1920.
On cooperation as a factor of evolution.

Schaffner, Bertram. *Father Land*. Columbia University Press, New York, 1948.
A study of authoritarianism in the German family.

Simpson, George Gaylord. *The Meaning of Evolution.* Yale University Press, 1949. New Haven, Conn.

By far the best book on the subject.

Suttie, Ian D. *The Origins of Love and Hate.* Kegan Paul, London, 1935.

A remarkable work on human nature, and a profoundly important corrective to Freud.

Tuker, M. A. R. *Past & Future of Ethics.* Oxford University Press, London, 1938.

A highly original and penetrating discussion of human nature and conduct.

Waddington, C. H. *The Ethical Animal.* Atheneum, New York, 1961.

On the framework within which our ethical beliefs should be evaluated and criticized.

INDEX

Abbott, D., 87n
Adler, Alfred, on cooperation and social feeling, 80–81, 84, 85–86; in newborn's relationship with mother, 53–54
Adorno, T. W., 91n
African Genesis, 44
Aggregation (*see also* Social appetite): vs. isolation, 37–46
Aggressiveness; aggression, 41ff, 89, 116 (*see also* Competition; Survival); deprived children and, 61ff
Ainsworth, M. D., 60n
Alexander, F., 54n
All Fools, 95
Allee, W. C., 41, 45; and cooperation among simple plants, animals, 37–39; on man's tendency to cooperation, goodness, 40
Allport, Floyd H., 70n
Allport, Gordon, 107n
Amoebae: reproduction of, 28, 29; and social appetite, cooperation, 32, 33
Animals (*see also* Survival): and aggregation vs. isolation, 37–42ff; and social appetite, 27–34
Ants, social, 42
Anxiety, 71–72
Apes, 76
Ardrey, Robert, 44
Ascent of Man, The, 26
Australian aborigines, 86–87
Automata, men as, 70–71

Bacteria, 33
Bakwin, Ruth M. and Harry, 56, 57
Banham, K. M., 90n
Barzini, Luigi, 67n
Bates, M., 87n
Bellevue Hospital (New York), 57

Bender, L., 41n, 89
Berelson, B., 13n
Berndt, R. M. and C. H., 87n
Bladder pressure, 50
Bogardus, Emory S., 69–70
Bonner, J. T., 33n
Boodin, John E., 75n
Bowlby, John, 60n
Bradbury, Ray, 71n
Brandes, George, 67n
Breathing, 50, 51
Brody, Sylvia, 65n
Bühler, Charlotte, 88–89
Burkholder, P. R., 43
Burns, J. H., 67n
Burrow, Trigant, 83, 84, 85

Capitalism, 101
Carthy, J. D., 41n
Casler, L., 60n
Caste, 116. *See also* Classes, social
Caterpillars, 32
Chapin, Henry D., 55n
Chapman, George, 95
Children. *See* Education; Infants and children
Christianity, 101
Classes, social, 116; and mothering, 64–67
Colon pressure, 50
"Combativeness," 41n. *See also* Aggressiveness
Communities. *See* Aggregation; Cooperation; Social appetite
Competition, 101, 108ff. *See also* Aggressiveness; Survival
"Conflict," 41n. *See also* Aggressiveness
Conformity, 91–92
Cooperation, 37–45, 73, 84ff, 100 (*see also* Dependency; Social appetite); Adler on (*see* Adler, Alfred); Darwin on, 21–22; and education in human rela-

125

127

Reproduction, 28–29*ff. See also* Sex; specific animals
Restlessness, 50
Ribble, Margaret, 57–60
Robertson, J. R., 55*n*
Rockefeller, John D., 20
Roheim, Geza, 76*n*
Romanell, P., 42*n*
Romanes Lecture, 18
Roosevelt, Franklin Delano, 110
Roux, Wilhelm, 31
Russians, 67. See also U.S.S.R.

Sanford, R. Nevitt, 91*n*
Sargent, S. S., 88*n*
Satisfaction. See Needs, man's
Sauvy, Alfred, 16*n*
Savages. See Nonliterate peoples
Schneirla, T. C., 42
Schools. See Education
Scott, J. P., 41*n*
Sea urchins, 38
Security, 77, 90, 98–99, 112 (*see also* Dependency; Love); infants and (*see* Infants and children)
Self, 73, 82–93, 94–95, 111–12. *See also* Egos; Individuality; Personality; Survival
Sex, 50; sexual reproduction, 28–29, 30
Shamanism, 74–75
Sharp, D. Louise, 108*n*
Sharpe, D. F., 89*n*
Sherrington, Sir Charles, 72–73
Sickness, 100. See also Neuroses
Simpson, George Gaylord, 31–32
"Sin," 88
Sinnott, Edmund W., 98*n*
Sleeping, 50
Smith, M. W., 88*n*
"Social," defined, 27
Social appetite, the, 27–35
Solitariness: aggregation vs. isolation, 37–46; infants and (*see* Infants and children); the social appetite, 27–35

Somnolence, 50
Sorokin, Pitirim A., 67*n*
Southworth, R. T., 55*n*
Spencer, Herbert; Spencerians, 19, 23
Spinley, B. M., 65*n*
Spiritual values, 101
Spiritual victories, 99
Stefansson, V., 87*n*
Steiner, G., 13*n*
"Struggle for existence," 17, 40. *See also* Competition
Success, 108*ff*
Sullivan, Harry Stack, 79
Supernatural, the, 74–75
Survival; "survival of the fittest," 16–25, 40–45, 109*ff*
Suttie, Ian D., 97

Talmud, 112, 114
Teachers, 107, 111
Tennyson, Alfred, Lord, 18
Thaxter, and bacteria, 33
Thirst, 50
Thomas, E. M., 87*n*
Tinbergen, N., 41*n*
Totalitarianism, 70–71; personality types and, 120
Transference, phenomenon of, 78–79
Trout, 34
Tuker, M. A. R., 115*n*

U.S.S.R., 114. *See also* Russians

Values, 101, 108*ff*
Van Tieghem (scientist), 33

Waddington, C. H.
War, 19, 20
Ward, Lester, 25
Western societies, 83, 85, 99, 109; and mothering, 64–67
Wheeler, W. M., 31
White, Winston, 92*n*
Witchcraft, 75
Wood, Margaret M., 77*n*
Wynne-Edwards, V. C., *n*

128